In The Beginning
Biblical Sparks for a Child's Week

Vered Hankin
Kalman J. Kaplan
Amiram Raviv

Illustrations by Theresa Bramblett

Library of Congress Cataloging-in-Publication Data

The CIP data for this book can be found on the Library of Congress website (loc.gov).

978-1-62396-436-8 (paperback);
978-1-62396-437-5 (hardcover);
978-1-62396-438-2 (e-book).

Cover Design and Illustrations by Theresa Bramblett

Copyright © 2013 Information Age Publishing Inc.

All rights reserved. No part of this publication may be reproduced, stored in a
retrieval system, or transmitted, in any form or by any means, electronic, mechanical, photocopying,
microfilming, recording or otherwise, without written permission
from the publisher.

Printed in the United States of America

The Community and
Educational Studies Press
at the University of Miami

Dunspaugh-Dalton Community
and Educational Wellness Center

In The Beginning

Vered Hankin
Kalman J. Kaplan
Amiram Raviv

Illustrations by Theresa Bramblett

INFORMATION AGE PUBLISHING, INC.
Charlotte, NC • www.infoagepub.com

To my little sparks:
   Jonah, Coral, and Julian.
                                    Vered Hankin

To my two beloved grandsons:
   Levi Judah and Isaiah Max.
                   Kalman J. Kaplan ("Grandpa Kal")

To my grandchildren:
   Tamar, Maya, Hadar, Leann, and Neta.
                                  Amiram Raviv

Table of Contents
In the Beginning: Biblical Sparks for a Child's Week

Introduction   1

DAY 1: **David and Goliath**
God Creates Form from Formlessness, Separates Light from Darkness   9

DAY 2: **The Tower of Babel**
God Separates Heaven from Earth   19

DAY 3: **Noah and the Flood**
God Separates Water from Dry Land   31

DAY 4: **Abraham and Idols**
God Creates the Sun and the Moon   43

DAY 5: **Jonah and the Great Fish**
God Creates the Birds, Sea Creatures, and Insects   55

DAY 6: **Adam Names the Animals**
God Gives Man Dominion over All Other Living Creatures   71

DAY 7: **The Sabbath:**
The Prophet Elijah Rests and Recovers His Strength
God Rests on the Sabbath, and Human Beings Need to Rest Also   85

Conclusions   101

Appendix   105

Bibliography   124

Introduction

Known as the "book of books," the Bible is the most successful bestselling book of all times. It lays the foundations for the worldview and moral stance of followers of all monotheistic religions. Beyond its religious significance and its contribution to the faith in one God, the Hebrew Scriptures present a framework that provides meaning and value to human existence in our world. The Bible provides guidance to people and suggests responses to crisis situations that are inevitable in human life. For the religious and non-religious alike, the Bible constitutes an important source of cultural heritage, worldviews, fundamental values, and basic codes of social conduct and personal beliefs. What is the secret of the Bible's perpetual appeal and the value attributed to it by so many individuals? The Bible presents the entire range of human characteristics, positive and negative. No human emotion or feeling, no matter how difficult or complex, is foreign to the Bible. Examination of the stories and contents of the Bible reveals their interest to people of all ages and across the ages. Thousands of years old, the stories continue to resonate with us, deepening our self-awareness and awareness of those around us.

Day of Week	Theme of Creation	Story
One	God creates form from formlessness, light from darkness, day from night. Evening comes before morning. (Genesis 1:1-5)	*David and Goliath* The lithe David defeats the clumsy Goliath. (I Samuel 17)
Two	God separates waters above (Heaven) from waters below (Earth). (Genesis 1:6-8)	*The Tower of Babel* Mankind is scattered for not respecting the division between earth and heaven. (Genesis 11)
Three	God separates dry land (Earth) from waters (Seas) and creates vegetation. (Genesis 1:9-13)	*Noah and the Flood* Mankind's immorality causes God to obliterate this separation. (Genesis 6-9)
Four	God creates two lights in the sky: The sun for day and the moon for night. (Genesis 1:14-19)	*Abraham Breaks the Idols* Abraham breaks the idols in his father's house and realizes that neither the sun nor moon should be worshiped. (Sefer Ha-Agadah 3:4,8)
Five	God creates birds, sea creatures, and insects (living creatures that creep). (Genesis 1:20-23)	*Jonah and the Big Fish* Jonah is saved from drowning when he is swallowed by a big fish. (Jonah)
Six	God creates land animals and human beings (male and female), the human beings in the likeness of God, and gives human beings dominion over all other living creatures. (Genesis 1:24-28)	*Adam Names the Animals* God brings the creatures he has created to Adam so he would name them. (Genesis 2:18)
Sabbath	God rests, and human beings need to rest as well. (Genesis 2:1-4)	*Elijah Rests* The weary Elijah rests and eats to recover his strength to continue his mission. (I Kings 17-18)

Nevertheless, modern psychology and psychiatry have made relatively very little use of these materials, being based largely on a classical Greek view of mental life. Instead, much of traditional psychotherapy has been based on classical Greek foundation legends (for example, Oedipus, Electra, and Narcissus). This view unfortunately seems to carry the tragic vision of classical Greece into modern life. In this view, no real change is possible, whereas in the biblical stories, life is not tragic but hopeful, and people can and do change. The idea that people's lives are not determined and that people have free will to change things around them is essential in empowering people to fight for social justice, and to generally show concern for other people.[1]

In this book, we present seven biblical legends, ordered to the days of Creation. Just as God created the Earth in the biblical tales, so it is that we can create our own journeys, filled with insight, ingenuity, and compassion. These stories are listed in the table on page 2 (opposite). Each of these stories in our seven chapters has been adapted for children in elementary and middle school grades, though some of the points of discussion are applicable even for adolescents and adults. Each story will be followed by an "Inside the Sparks" section, consisting of commentaries and questions, designed to illuminate the material and make it applicable to children.

We suggest using these stories to deepen a child's understanding of the ebb and flow of life. Because the Bible addresses human emotions and human interactions, its stories seem to provide appropriate means of encouraging interest in and discussion of fundamental human issues, fostering social skills and living out humane and human values.

---

[1] Erich Wellisch (1954) eloquently called for a Biblical Psychology to free human beings from the determinisitic and tragic assumptions of ancient Greece so endemic to our contemporary models of mental health.

In recent years psychologists and educators have developed an interest in the concept of emotional intelligence (EQ).[2] The EQ approach emphasizes moral, attitudinal, and behavioral aspects that contribute to individuals' social adaptation, successful social integration, and general level of functioning. We will not discuss all aspects of EQ in detail, but will only mention a few of them: awareness of one's own emotions and a reasonable degree of emotional control; restraint and ability to delay gratification; empathy and sensitivity to others' feelings and consideration toward others; social skills, self-confidence, and confidence in others. All of these represent central components of EQ. This is a flexible and optimistic approach, fostering a milieu wherein people can feel good about themselves.

The developers of this approach believe that EQ skills can be nurtured from an early age, or learned in adulthood. In contrast to the concept of IQ, which is usually assumed to be determined at birth or to develop in early childhood, EQ can be acquired and cultivated throughout the life course. There is something flexible and optimistic about this approach, which sees opportunities for development and change.

Reading the Bible carefully highlights the educational purpose of biblical stories. They aim to nurture the human soul and improve people's behavior. In fact, the Bible conveyed psychological insights long before psychology became an established scientific discipline. Much of what we know about human nature today validates the insights expressed in the writings of our ancestors.

---

[2] The concept of EQ was introduced by Peter Salovey from Yale University and gained much popularity with the publication of Daniel Goleman's book Emotional Intelligence. The conceptual framework of emotional intelligence refers to a combination of various emotional and social skills and abilities. The contribution of this concept is an extension of the familiar concept of IQ. It suggests that persons with identical IQ levels may attain different achievements as a function of their emotional intelligence. IQ is important for success, but EQ is equally important.

There is no ancient book as applicable to modern times as the Bible. Biblical stories do not just teach abstract knowledge but also tell deeply human stories to nurture the human soul and improve people's behavior. First, we will recount the respective day of creation. Secondly, we present the story, retold in an animated and engaging style. Thirdly, we offer a brief psychological interpretation that highlights some of the themes of the story and clarifies messages nurturing various life skills. In our questions and commentary, we do not presume to suggest the only "true interpretation" possible, but rather hope to encourage multiple interpretations. We also do not propose to replace traditional interpretations developed over generations by religious authorities or erudite biblical scholars. Rather, we emphasize the points that could possibly be psychologically beneficial to children in order to provide an instrument that educators may use in their work with children.

The questions appearing after the stories are designed to facilitate understanding of the stories' contents and development of discussions of issues that the stories raise. Here, too, we have not intended to exhaust all the possibilities. The questions should be regarded as providing and stimulating discussion topics. They may provide an illustration for parents and educators of a dialectic approach, where asking questions and exploring ideas are more important than absolute answers. The questions, as well as the interpretations, are meant as teaching guides; parents may or may not choose to incorporate these into their reading time with their child.

The Stories
In the Beginning: Biblical Sparks for a Child's Week

DAY ONE: David and Goliath
God Shapes Form out of Formlessness, Separates Light from Darkness

In the beginning God created the heaven and the earth. Now the earth was unformed and void, and darkness was upon the face of the deep; and the spirit of God hovered over the face of the waters. And God said: "Let there be light." And there was light. And God saw the light, that it was good: and God divided the light from the darkness. And God called the light Day, and the darkness He called Night. And there was evening and there was morning, one day. (Genesis 1:1–5)

A long time ago, there was a young boy named David. David was the youngest of eight sons. He stayed home with his father and tended to the sheep, while several of his brothers were away, fighting in the Israelite army, against the Philistines.

One day, David's father announced: "David, I am worried about your brothers. After all, they are at war. What if something happens to them? I have a few things I want to send them—some fruits and vegetables, and some freshly baked bread. Please take these to them. I also have ten different kinds of cheese for you to give to their captain. Maybe if we give him these, he'll be extra nice to them. While you're there, find out how they're doing and bring me back the news. Don't forget to tell them I miss them and look forward to their coming home safely."

David was always happy to help. He was known for being fast, and so immediately he set off on his journey to meet his brothers. But as soon as he got to the battle site, David noticed worried looks on everyone's faces. "What is it?" he asked.

O

"They say that the Philistines have a soldier who is 9 feet tall!" they replied nervously. "Goliath is his name. They say his armor is so heavy that just the tip of his sword weighs over 20 pounds! He alone could destroy our entire army. We're in big trouble!"

David was concerned. If his father had been somewhat worried before, he would surely be worried now! How could he possibly deliver this news to him? Just then, there was a giant roar. Everyone turned around, and there on the top of the hill stood the tallest, biggest man David had ever seen. "Hello there, you little cowards!" Goliath roared. "I'll make you a deal. You send just one of your men—your strongest man—to fight me and maybe, just maybe I'll spare – well, at least a few of you! Hahaha!"

Everyone shuddered with fear, but David grew angry. Who is this man who dares speak to us in this way? "Hey everyone, don't forget that God is on our side. Please don't worry. We can overcome this challenge. He is big, but he is clumsy. I myself will fight this man!"

When the others heard this, they burst out laughing. "You? You're a kid!" they jeered.

Even David's brothers were upset with David. Perhaps his courage made them feel insecure. Whatever the reason, they made fun of him for his foolish bravery. "Hey, little Davie, give us the goodies our father sent us and run back home to Daddy. Tell him we can take care of ourselves. We don't need a snoop like you to bug us or pretend he's some kind of hero. Go home and tend to your sheep! That's the way you'll learn to be a man—by doing your job and staying in your place. Now go on, scram!"

But David was serious, and he didn't like to be made fun of. "I will! I will fight this man. If nobody else will, I will protect our people! I am not afraid!"

"Not afraid?" One of the soldiers overheard him and was impressed by David's courage. "We're all terrified! How is a little guy like you not scared? Well, I can't imagine that the king would ever let you fight the giant Goliath— but if you want to come with us we can see what he has to say!"

David was brought to the palace, and when King Saul saw him, he too began to laugh. "Do tell me, young man, what is your grand plan?"

"I don't need much of a plan," David announced to King Saul. "God is with the Israelite people and God will be with me. How dare this bully try to intimidate us?"

King Saul shook his head. "Young man, you are just a boy. You don't have the strength or the experience to fight in any army, let alone to fight the biggest and most fearsome giant in the land. Go on home!"

"With all due respect, King Saul," David insisted. "I DO have experience. Not with people, it's true, but I have fought some of the most dangerous beasts in the land."

"Really? How so?" King Saul asked with a smile.

"Well, many times, when I've been watching my sheep, a lion has come in search of its dinner. I have personally grabbed my sheep out of the jaws of a lion. Once, when the lion came after me, I took him by its mane and killed him. I have done the same with bears. If I can fight them, I can and I will fight this man."

King Saul was impressed. He was also desperate, for no other soldiers were willing to fight Goliath. They were too scared. "Young man, do you understand how dangerous this mission is?"

"Yes, King Saul, I do."

"If you are indeed willing to take on the challenge, I will allow you to fight."

David was both excited and nervous. Immediately, the king's soldiers brought out a beautiful brass suit of armor. This would protect him from the giant's weapons. But when little David tried on the suit, he was too small to wear it! The armor was so big that one suit pant leg could have fit little David's whole body—and the iron mask reached his knees! David decided he would go without armor. The armor would keep him from moving freely; it would just slow him down. "After all," he kept telling himself, "God is on my side." At this point, David had no choice but to move forward. He walked outside in search of a weapon. He had his slingshot with him, and once he found five good stones, David was ready to go.

The next day everyone gathered around to watch the young and small David take on the giant Goliath. What would happen to little David? Giant Goliath towered above on one hill, whereas tiny David could barely be seen on the next. Goliath squinted over towards David. When he saw that his opponent was merely an unarmored young boy, he laughed. "You are the one I am slated to fight?" His voice boomed. "A young boy?! A little puppy? Ha! Who do you think I am? A dog who can be forced to 'sit' or 'stay' with a single stick or stone? So, you wish to fight me. Well, come on, little boy. I'll tell you what: I'll give you the first punch. Ha! I will send you flying into the air so fast you won't even be able to say…"

But as Goliath was laughing, David was concentrating. "You may be a big bully," he proclaimed, "but God is on our side!" Swiftly, David grabbed a small stone and flung it with his slingshot as hard as he could—right at Goliath's head. The stone flew straight between Goliath's eyes, lodging itself right in his forehead with a thump. Goliath fell down instantly.

When the Philistines saw that Goliath had been defeated, they all ran away in fear. The Israelites celebrated and pronounced David their hero. King Saul was so impressed that he asked David to come live with him and be as a son to him. Saul had another son, Jonathan, and Jonathan and David soon became best of friends. Everyone in the land spoke highly of David's bravery, and David soon became known as the best warrior in the whole army—and the most beloved. In fact, it was David's bravery, strength, and honesty that eventually led him to become the next king of Israel.

Inside the Sparks

The story of the fight between David and Goliath is a prototypical story of a struggle between the weak and the strong, in which the seemingly weak party eventually manages to prevail over the strong one against all odds. Like most biblical stories, this story conveys the message that faith in God is rewarded and that believers receive the assistance that they need in order to overcome their seemingly stronger enemies. In addition, the story demonstrates that determination, faith, wisdom, and creativity can overcome brute physical strength.

The story contains many important themes that may be discussed with children and students, both at home and in educational settings. We address some of the most salient themes in the sample questions presented below; indeed, these themes may be further developed and expanded.

David fortuitously arrives at the scene of the battle. His father sends him with provisions for his brothers. He hears Goliath's denigration and witnesses the helplessness in Saul's camp. When he audaciously volunteers to fight the Philistine, his brothers are upset with him (presumably because his courage makes them feel inferior and nervous) and confront him for abandoning the flock. This may provide an opportunity to discuss relationships between older and younger siblings, when the latter are daring and successful. Yet, this is obviously a minor theme of the plot.

Goliath's character vividly demonstrates the limitations of an inflexible strength and obtuse vanity. He is depicted as a rigid bully. To lend further support to this characterization, he also degrades and humiliates his opponents. This provides an opportunity to discuss issues of pride and vanity.

What sort of needs do they serve? Perhaps they are actually indications of insecurity? How do we evaluate others and ourselves? By which criteria? What is the difference between self-confidence and overconfidence? Goliath's main failings are his awkwardness and his underestimation of others, leading to a misjudgment of the situation and eventually to his death.

Goliath initially frightens his opponents, who as a result are at a loss. The young and untrained David arrives with a different motivation and outlook on the situation. He believes in his ability to defeat Goliath. When King Saul questions David's ability to withstand Goliath, David tells Saul about his success in fighting animals that harassed his flock. Being so desperate, Saul succumbs to David's pleas and attempts to reduce the risk of injury by offering David a heavy armor. Realizing that his advantage lies in his flexibility and agility, David declines the offer. One can interpret the latter as a metaphor for the advantage of flexibility over rigidity as a life strategy. This provides an opportunity to develop a discussion about the value of creativity, creative problem solving, and overcoming rigid conventions. David's agility and litheness in contrast to Goliath's hulking awkwardness illustrates the theme of the first day of Creation—the advance from formlessness to form and from darkness to light.

Questions

1. How do David's brothers react when David volunteers to fight Goliath?
2. How do the Israelites react to Goliath's proposition? What do they fear?
3. What does Goliath think about himself?
4. What is unique about David's approach? How is he different from Goliath?
5. Why was David not afraid, in your opinion? What helped him prevail?
6. What makes a person courageous? Is a person who does not recognize danger courageous?
7. Why is vanity considered a negative quality?
8. What is the difference between vanity and self-confidence?
9. Which qualities help us cope with problems? What is the advantage of light versus darkness, form versus formlessness?
10. Why is it important to be flexible? What are the disadvantages of being rigid?

DAY TWO: The Tower of Babel
God Separates Heaven from Earth

And God said: "Let there be a firmament in the midst of the waters and let it divide the waters from the waters. And God made the firmament, and divided the waters which were under the firmament from the waters which were above the firmament: and it was so. And God called the firmament Heaven. And there was evening and there was morning, a second day. (Genesis 1: 6–8)

A few years after the great flood, there was only one group of people on the earth. They had a great deal. They had all the food and drink they wanted. They had a beautiful place to live. Furthermore, they were able to communicate with each other, all speaking one language, with one set of customs and traditions. God was in the heavens, and they were on the earth. God watched over them and saw that their life was good. God commanded them to have many children and populate the earth.

One day, one of them began to wonder: "It's so nice how all of us are one big wonderful family. We understand each other. We love and respect one another. It's perfect! But wait a moment: what if we really do go out and populate the entire earth? What if there are so many of us we can no longer stay together? Maybe some of us will wish to settle in faraway lands? We might even learn to speak, think, and act differently. We may eventually grow apart. Perhaps we may eventually lose respect for each other. Is it possible that some of us may even wish to fight each other?" The man tried to shake off these thoughts as "just nonsense." But the more he tried to fight the

thoughts, the stronger and more powerful they seemed to grow, until soon it was all he could think about.

He did not trust God to take care of him and his people. He feared God would disperse them around the world. He even began to resent the fact that God lived in heaven while they lived on earth. Why could they not live in heaven as well? Who was God anyhow? Why could they not be like God? Why could they not be God themselves? Nervously, he gathered the entire group together. "Everyone, I must tell you. I used to be happy, just like the rest of you. But lately, I've begun to worry. I worry and worry and worry all the time! Why should God be in the heavens and we on earth?"

"Why, everything is just perfect as it is," one elder proclaimed with a peaceful smile. "Whatever could be worrying you? Things are as they should be. God is in heaven where God belongs, and we are on earth. It is just as it should be."

The man explained his resentment and his ambition. Even though they were happy now, who knew what the future could bring? Why should they not control the heavens as well as earth? Why were they limited to earth?

"Please," the elder comforted. "Let's let well enough alone. If things are good now, why worry about the future? Let's just enjoy the present."

"Why worry?!" the man replied. "You never know what could happen! It is imperative that we not depend on God and take power for ourselves!"

Suddenly, one man pushed through the crowd. "I have it! I have it!" the man proclaimed. "It's true that if we remain unaware we might be taken care of, but we are still dependent. Why don't we take power for ourselves? What if God no longer pays attention to us? We have no control over our lives, but we can get control. It is in the heavens. I believe in our power!"

Everyone cheered, and the man continued, "Look up to the sky. What do you see? The heavens?" Everyone nodded and whispered in agreement. "Yes, the heavens. There is a God up there in the sky who wants us to think that God makes the rules. God tells us when we live and when we die. Who we are and what we do. No more of that! WE will decide where the heaven ends and where the earth begins. WE will wage war on God, show God who's boss, and that way we know that nobody will mess with us, and nobody will separate us." The crowd cheered wildly, as the man continued, "So now, each of you take a brick and begin to build the tallest building in the sky. And on the top we'll place a giant statue with a big sword in its hand, and this will send the message to God that WE not only rule the earth but the heavens as well!"

The entire crowd cheered. Immediately, each person grabbed a brick. They prepared mortar and began to build. Higher and higher their building rose. They were so excited to build it—their sanctuary, their protection against all harm.

But as the building grew taller and taller, the building process became more and more dangerous. Some of the older members grew tired and needed to rest, but others forced them to keep on working. If someone fell, nobody noticed, but if a brick fell they cried: "Oh, all that work! Now it will take so much longer!"

When God saw this, God grew very disappointed. God's people trying to wage war against God—a ridiculous endeavor—but they were also being nasty to each other. By focusing so much on what they didn't have, and by

being so greedy and dissatisfied, these people had completely ignored all the joys they did have in their life. Here they were trying to take over the heavens, when they didn't even know how to manage themselves on earth.

"Well, I know what it is that they most fear," God spoke. "In a way they have already created it. They will only cultivate anger and sadness. They are creating the very event they had feared!"

God knew there was only one way to stop them from moving forward and completely destroying each other. With a heavenly wave, God mixed up their languages. Soon, one was speaking French, while the other began speaking Japanese. One thought the other was asking for water and gave him a brick, while the other thought his friend was asking for a brick and gave him water. Another asked to borrow a mule and was given a pitcher of milk. A third asked for a pitcher of milk and was given a chicken. A fourth person asked for a chicken and was given a dog. And finally, a fifth person asked for a ride and was given a cat. It was a real mess. Nobody understood anyone.

They became frustrated with each other. Angry. Soon, they couldn't work together at all. One by one, they gave up. Since they couldn't understand each other anymore, each went on his way, and they became dispersed all over the earth. Indeed, since each spoke a different language and learned to act differently, they began to develop different customs and even values. Soon, they grew to grossly misunderstand each other, with some eventually even declaring war against each other.

The tower that they had intended to build was thus named "The Tower of Babel" because "babel" means confusion. Indeed, God had confounded their languages, making it impossible for them to ever complete the tower that was to invade the heavens. So, too, were they confused in their intentions.

Rather than embrace all that was wonderful in their lives, they were greedy for more. When their greed increased, they were no longer satisfied with earth but wanted to go up to the heavens. No longer trusting God, they looked outside for power. They forgot that they were God's precious creation. They lost the strength of their hearts to keep them connected, respectful and grateful for the seamless and magical boundaries between heaven and earth. By wanting too much, they wound up with less and brought about the very thing they feared.

Inside the Sparks

The story of the construction of the Tower of Babel offers an explanation for the multiplicity and diversity of languages among the nations of the world. The message that the Bible intends to convey in the story is very clear: humans should not challenge divine creation. Even intelligent and industrious people should not be so filled with their own self-importance that they believe that they can prevail over their Creator. Impudence and provocation lead to punishment.

Besides the theological message, the story also contains significant indicators of the nature of human behavior and raises issues that may be discussed with children in order to convey important insights regarding social interactions.

We elaborate here on four salient themes in the story.

1. ***The element of pride – hubris***: The defiance of God, beyond the religious issue of heresy, symbolizes defiance and protest against superiors. The discussion may address situations in which people may become frustrated with their superiors. Things may become even more complicated if those superiors are those that encouraged and nurtured the person. Behaviors that are ungrateful toward one's benefactors may also be discussed. Yet in some cases, frustration may develop due to a sense of limitation and denial of the freedom of choice.

   The implications to relationships between parents and children are quite clear. How can a child cope with such frustration? How can a child express protest? Are there other ways of achieving and expressing independence? Protest and rebellion may be risky. What about excessive ambition, which may propel us to take uncalculated risks?

However, in addition to addressing the negative aspects of such behavior, one may also examine its positive side. Aspirations and ambitions drive achievements. The accomplishments of human civilization and science would not have been achieved without ambition and initiative. Children are expected to "spread their wings" and leave their parents' custody eventually. Yet they are always supposed to honor their parents. It is the same with human beings and God. It is important to take on challenges, face difficulties, and develop an ability to organize and recruit alliances in order to promote complex projects. But it is always important for people to have a sense of modesty about their creative gifts and realize that they are beneficiaries of these gifts and must use them for positive ends, rather than to build up their power.

2. *The importance of interpersonal communication*: The story conveys this lesson through negation. In punishment of hubris, God mixes the languages of the construction workers (in Hebrew the word "balal" means "to mix", and the text suggests that this is the Hebrew

source for the name Babel). When God wishes to thwart human intentions, God disrupts a central God-given gift—communication.

In the beginning, construction of the tower could progress efficiently because everyone involved spoke one language and could communicate with each other to achieve coordination and harmony. When each person spoke a different language, chaos ensued. This is an illustration of the concept of "misunderstanding." The parable demonstrates that nothing can be organized or constructed when the persons involved cannot communicate. The story teaches the importance of listening to others and making an effort to understand what they are saying and what they mean.

This lesson is important even in societies where everyone speaks the same language. Differences of opinion, disagreements, and misunderstandings are possible in every society, and they may occasionally lead people to behave as though they do not understand each other at all despite speaking the same language. Perhaps they are unable or unwilling to understand fully what others are saying. Thus, one of the important lessons is that in order to maintain a social structure, harmony, and quality of life, we must foster everyone's interpersonal communication skills with an emphasis on empathy, which means attempting to understand the feelings of others.

Tolerance of others' opinions and the ability to listen patiently and to express ideas clearly and comprehensibly are essential elements of communication in a given society. It may also be possible to elaborate the discussion of means that may enable members of different nations, who speak different languages, to communicate with each other.

3. *The importance of trust.* The story illustrates the potentially corrosive and destructive implications of the failure to trust. By not trusting God, the people try to make a name for themselves by becoming gods themselves. They thus bring about the dispersion they had been trying to prevent. It is very important for a child to know whom to trust and whom to distrust. Undiscerning trust can put a child in great danger. However, a pervasive mistrust may lead to an equal if not greater danger and may lead a child into a situation he is trying to avoid.

Teaching a child when to trust is a formidable task for a parent. A parent may tell a child to answer the phone when the parent is absent with a vague response such as " my mother is not available right now" rather than to say "my mother is not home." Such caution is wise in contemporary society. At the same time, in order to make real progress, a child must be able to trust a parent, a teacher, a coach, a group leader. Otherwise, the child may be in a constant state of rebellion, which could keep him from those trying to instruct him or even protect him. The story of the Tower of Babel may provide a foundation for any

educational program that attempts to convey the values of understanding and tolerance among members of a social group and between different groups and societies. With older students, one may elaborate the discussion to encompass problems of modern urban societies, which include alienation, difficulties of communications, and barriers to forming relationships among members of a given society and between members of various social and economic strata, particularly marginal groups.

4. *The fear of separation.* The story finally illustrates the terrible problems that occur due to fear of separation. Genesis recounts how one God separates heaven from earth, land from water, day from night, man from woman. These separations and differentiations can all be tolerated because one God has created the universe. They are not the same thing as non-relatedness and estrangement. When people begin to fear normal individuation, separation, and differentiation, they stop trusting God and try to replace God in the heavens. This leads to their being estranged from one another. They bring about what they are trying to avoid.

Questions

1. Why did the people want to build a tower that would reach the sky? What were they afraid of?
2. What was the sin of the builders? Why was God angry with them?
3. Why was the construction of the tower not completed?
4. Why is it important to understand each other?
5. What are the advantages of being able to speak more than one language?
6. What happens when people who speak different languages meet? What can they do in order to communicate with each other?
7. Can you describe a situation where two people speak the same language and still do not understand each other?
8. What is the difference between being a separate person and being estranged from other people?
9. Do you sometimes bring about what you are trying to avoid? When does this happen?
10. What does it mean to make a name for yourself? Is it important for you to do this? How does it make you feel?

DAY THREE: Noah and the Flood
God Separates Water from Dry Land

> *And God said: "Let the waters under the heavens be gathered together unto one place, and let the dry land appear. And it was so. And God called the dry land Earth and the gathering of the waters called The Seas. And God said: "Let the earth put forth grass, herb yielding seed, and fruit-tree bearing fruit after its kind, wherein is the seed thereof, upon the earth." And it was so. And the earth brought forth grass, herb yielding seed after its kind, and tree bearing fruit, wherein is the seed thereof, after its kind; and God saw that it was good. And there was evening and there was morning, a third day.* (Genesis 1:9–13)

It was a tough time for God. After all God's work in creating the Earth, the sky, and the water, and separating one from the other, people seemed to lose their connection to God and God's creatures, and being created uniquely in the divine image. They lost respect for themselves and they lost respect for others as well. They soon started being mean to each other. Really mean, and wicked. They had lost their connection to a very important piece inside of them—gratitude. Because they were no longer thankful, they began mistreating animals, littering and ruining the Earth, and stealing from the land. They no longer trusted God's plan. They had lost their way.

God saw this, and felt the emptiness in the land. God missed their prayers of thanks and for help or guidance. "Maybe," God thought, "maybe there is someone there calling to me, asking me for help in finding thanks, in finding joy."

God listened very carefully. But there was only silence—the wooshing of the wind, the chirping of the birds.

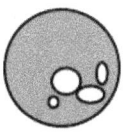

"I'm here to help!" God announced. "Anybody have a prayer for me?"

A tiny voice rang towards the heavens. No, it was a group of voices. A community searching for help? God zoomed down, looking for the source.

A home. One home. One family. A family with smiles, with love, open hearts. Helping each other, feeding and caring for their animals, watering the garden—not trampling it. Calling out their thanks to the creator of the world. God took in a sigh of relief. "Music to my ears. Somebody appreciates. Ahhhhh…"

But the moment God looked around outside of this home, people were pushing each other, yelling at each other, cheating each other. "Enoooooooouuuuuuuuuuuuugh!" God roared. A single clash of thunder hit the perfectly still sunny sky.

One of the men in the happy hut, Noah, poked his head out. "Could rain be coming?" He looked up towards the sky. "Nahhh!" He shook his head and stepped back in to help his wife prepare dinner.

God knew what had to be done. "I created people to be helpful and loving, not to be horrible to each other. Why can't they be more like Noah and his family? You know, I think it's time to destroy the Earth and start anew. A cleanse. A clean break. I created the world once. I can do it again—but I only want people to come out of Noah's family, to learn to be like them. Kind. Respectful. Grateful to be alive."

God thought for a moment. Perhaps there was another way? A prayer in the distance? "One more chance. Do I hear anything…?" The sound of a gushing waterfall filled God's ears. "Water. Beautiful endless flowing water. Sustainer of life. One of my best creations." God thought for a moment. "Wait! That's just it! Water! I will use the very sustenance of life to destroy life. Start anew.

I separated water from land in the third day of my creation. Now I will mix them together again to try to correct what has gone wrong. I'll erase the world and start from Noah. Perfect. Peerrrrrrrrrffffffffffffffffffect!" Another clash of thunder sounded, but everyone was too busy arguing to notice.

Except for Noah, who poked out his head. "Rain? No. Couldn't be. It's not the rain season!" He was just about to step back inside when he heard something a bit different.

"Nooooooooooooooah!" Noah poked his head out again. What was that? "Noah. It's me. You know, the force that created you."

"I hear you but I can't see you. What did you say your name was?"

"Look, I don't want to brag or anything, but you pretty much know me for one of my biggest inventions, if you will."

"Mortar and pestle?"

"Um, well, yeah, indirectly I guess. But I was really talking about the creator of ... or as some of my fans like to call me, 'Master' of the universe. You know, ME."

Noah shuddered. Could it be true? Could this be... God? Noah was stunned. "Master of the universe, your wish is my command. How can I be of service?"

God smiled. Now THIS was gratitude. "Oh Noah, my child, go forth and build an ark."

"An ARK?"

"You know, a big giant boat. And I do mean GIANT boat. I need you to be able to fit animals in there—lots of animals."

"Um, which animals?"

"ALL animals. Well, seven males and seven females of each animal. Except for non-kosher animals. We only want two males and females of those."

"Are people going to be on it too?"

"Oh yes, but just your family. Nobody else."

"You mean like a private cruise?"

"Well, sort of. You see, Noah, you guys are my favorites."

"Your favorites? Wow, God, I don't know what to say. I'm so touched. I…"

"Yeah, yeah, listen. No time for the mushy stuff. It's time to start building. I'll give you the exact dimensions, and I'll provide the guest list. But you must start — NOW!"

Noah did begin right away. Although his wife supported his work, she shook her head: "Six hundred years old. When are you going to retire?"

"Right after this project, honey," Noah assured her, and soon he had a giant ark, just as God had requested, filled with food. Two by two and seven by seven the animals made their way to the ark. As Noah and his family began to pack, people came by to make fun of them and to steal the belongings they were leaving behind. But Noah's family didn't stray from their mission. They, too, made their way onto the ark.

"Now what?" Shem, his oldest son asked. "Where is this ark supposed to go?"

"It'll soon become clear." Noah responded. "For now, we will wait."

"It's tiiiiiiiiiiiiiiiiiiiiiiiiiiime!" God roared, and a clash of thunder shook the land. "I can seeeeeeee it!" God exclaimed, and lightning lit up the sky. "Ready, Noah, get set for a forty-day vacation!!!!!!!!!!!!!!!"

Immediately, it began to pour. It rained and rained and rained. So much so that soon the ark was floating. Homes, farms, people, animals were all covered by the sea. But Noah's family and the animals in the ark were all safe above the growing waters. It was a miracle. And Noah was ever so grateful to be alive.

After forty days of rain, Noah needed to know if it was safe to leave the ark. "I will go search for dry land," the raven announced, and Noah sent him forth. But the raven never returned.

"Now what?" Noah wondered.

"Oh, Noah," cooed the dove. "I am not as big or brave as the raven, but I can fly, and I would be honored to search for you." Noah sent out the dove, who soon returned empty-handed. A week later he sent her out again. This time she returned with an olive branch in her beak. Noah then sent the dove out a third time, and she did not return. Noah then knew the water was no longer covering the earth. It was time to leave the ark.

The rain had indeed stopped, and Noah, his family, and all the animals found their place on dry land. Noah thanked God for his life.

Just then Noah noticed something—a beautiful and majestic multi-colored bow in the sky. "Wow!" Noah exclaimed.

"Yeah, I know," God replied. "I'm good. But you know what? You're pretty good too. And your family. There will be many generations after you, and I know there might be times I might become angry at you or at your children, or grandchildren. But I'll always remember your gratitude towards me, and I promise I will never destroy my creations like that again. This bow in the sky—we'll call it a 'rainbow' because it will appear in the sky after it rains. It's a reminder to you and to all people and animals that the rain will stop and I will never destroy my people again."

Noah and his family were sure happy to hear that, as were the animals. And so are we too, you know. It's good to know that we've got a relationship with God, and a beautiful rainbow to always remind us of it.

Inside the Sparks

The story of the flood illustrates quite well the theme of the third day of creation: the separation of water from dry land. This separation is essential to human life. When this separation is violated, as in floods, human life may be jeopardized. The Bible sees the flood as punishment to the humans for their sins. The construction of the ark by the righteous Noah and the salvation of humankind and wildlife is a complex and fascinating story that encompasses many themes. We mention some of these themes of the story that may be elaborated in a discussion with children or adolescents.

Beyond the religious implications of the issue of sin and punishment, which is at the heart of the story, its discussion may elaborate the meaning of drastic punishment and expand to address issues of punishment and retribution in human society as well as proportionality between transgression and punishment. The discussion need not be limited by the fact that the original story is somewhat vague regarding the human sins.

A related aspect is the righteous character of Noah. The story contrasts the evil persons that must be punished with the righteous man that must be saved. What does it mean to be righteous? What does society expect from a righteous person? With older students, the discussion may be elaborated to address the issue of altruism and factors that may lie behind altruistic behavior.

In general, the story may be discussed with older children at a higher level of abstraction. One of the most meaningful acts of creation was the separation between the waters below and the waters above, which are the heavens. The Book of Genesis emphasizes separations made by God: day from night, heaven from earth, earth from the seas, and man from woman. In the story of the flood, God violates this order by bringing the flood water down on the earth. One may discuss the importance of order and boundary-setting in the universe. What are the advantages of order and boundaries? What are their limitations? Order may refer to the environment around us or to our inner selves. Sometimes it is important to introspective and put our thoughts and feelings in order.

The story of the flood eventually emphasizes the new order and God's commitment not to apply such severe sanctions again. The rainbow is a symbol of God's commitment and promise. What do we know about the significance of giving one's word, or of taking a commitment or obligation upon ourselves? Why are commitments and obligations important for the maintenance of social order?

At the concrete level, the story provides examples for considerations taken regarding generational perpetuation. The animals are selected based on a plan and considerations of succession. All animals are expected to proliferate, and there is a place for all kinds in the world. In this context, the discussion may emphasize issues of tolerance and everyone's right to exist. One may address elements such as acceptance of others and consideration. Imagine what life on the ark would have been like with all the different animals and their different needs and interests without consideration and tolerance.

With respect to animals, one may also discuss ecological issues, referring to the importance of preserving nature and being considerate of wildlife. As humans, we have been trusted with the task of preserving our planet, lest we give rise to another man-made flood due to being inconsiderate toward our environment.

Returning to the rainbow, it may also be seen as a symbol for the coexistence of all colors together, with no single color dominant over the others. The rainbow is a sign of the covenant between God and humans, but it may also symbolize a covenant among humans.

Finally, the dove returning with an olive branch has become a symbol for the human aspiration for peace. However, despite the almost universal desire for peace, numerous wars continue to be waged around the world. What can be done in order to foster peace and prevent war? It is important to encourage children to be aware of this issue and to motivate them to seek solutions, especially regarding conflicts in their close environment and with other children. Perhaps when they grow up they may continue to apply what they learned in other settings.

Questions

1. Why did God bring the flood upon the earth?

2. Why did God command Noah to build an ark? What was Noah asked to do? Why?

3. Why did Noah find grace in the eyes of God?

4. What does the rainbow symbolize? What can we learn from it?

5. Why did God want male and female of each species to go on the ark?

6. What do we mean when we say that someone is righteous? What do righteous people do? How do they behave?

7. Why is it important to avoid hurting animals?

8. God gets very angry but eventually brings about a rainbow to promise he will never do it again. Can you make up with someone you were angry with?

9. How do you feel when your friends disappoint you?

10. Can you see the good in people even when you are angry with them?

DAY FOUR: Abraham and Idols
God Creates the Sun and the Moon

And God said: "Let there be lights in the firmament of the heaven to divide the day from the night; and let them be for signs, and for seasons, and for days and years: and let them be for lights in the firmament of the heaven to give light upon the earth. And it was so. And God made the two great lights: the greater light to rule the day, and the lesser light to rule the night, and the stars. And God set them in the firmament of the heavens to give light upon the earth. And to rule over the day and over the night, and to divide the light from the darkness; and God saw that it was good. And there was evening and there was morning, a fourth day. (Genesis 1:14–19)

Once, a long time ago there was a young boy named Abram. Abram's father was very wealthy, and everyone in the land looked up to him. His father had a beautiful store, full of life-size sculptures in the image of animals and people. Everyone from all over the land would shop at this store, and everyone wanted a sculpture. Why, you might ask, did everyone want a sculpture? Nowadays only a very few people have them, perhaps as a decoration in their living room or in their front or backyard. You may see them in museums or as monuments decorating some city streets. But back then, things were different. You see, these sculptures weren't just for decoration. No, back then, people believed that these sculptures were gods. They would bow down to them and pray to them, ask them for favors, and plead with them to keep bad things from happening.

Abram didn't like this idea much. How was it possible, he thought, that the statue could be a god? After all, people made statues, and more than once he had seen a statue at his father's shop break an arm or a leg. Certainly, a real god would never have a broken arm! But everyone around Abram thought differently, especially his father.

One day, Abram's father had to leave on a business trip, "Abram!" he commanded. "I need you to watch the store. As you know, these sculptures are very precious. Make sure nothing happens to them. I trust you to take good care of them. I will be back soon and will count on you to keep everything in its place!"

Abram felt uncomfortable. How could he take such care of these sculptures when he knew they were not gods at all? Suddenly, Abram had a clever idea. He grabbed a big heavy stick and began smashing the sculptures, one by one—all except for the biggest one. That particular statue stood strong with its arms stretched out as if it was about to grab something. Abram placed the stick into the statue's arm, so it appeared as if the statue was holding it. "Perfect!" Abram snickered.

When Abram's father returned from his trip, he arrived to see the store filled with smashed sculptures. He was horrified. "Abram! What happened here? My entire store is in shambles! How could you let this happen? Who did this?!"

"Why, Father," Abram calmly replied. "I am in shock as well. See that big statue? HE did it!"

Abram's father looked at Abram with piercing eyes and a bright red face: "Abram, do you expect me to believe that a statue could move and take a stick and smash all these other statues?! Statues cannot do that! They are not alive!!!"

"You're right, father," Abram calmly replied. "They are not alive. They are not able to move or to act or to do much of anything, so why would we pray to them as if they were gods?!"

Abram knew how angrily his father sometimes reacted, and he was afraid. Quickly, Abram galloped off. If it was true that the statues were not gods, well then, what was? That's when Abram noticed it—the sun! It shone so brightly he could hardly believe it. A beautiful day! Of course, the sun was God—after all, it made the flowers grow, it brought light and warmth. He had found God. Immediately, Abram began to pray: "Thank you, sun, for all of the wonderful gifts you have given us—for the beautiful plants and flowers that you make grow, for our ability to see during the day, for shining upon us and keeping us warm. Thank you, sun!!!"

Abram continued praying all day long, until… evening came. The sun began to fall. Beautiful colors lit up the sky, but soon—the sun was gone. "God wouldn't come and go like that. Wait, maybe God is not the sun at all, but—the moon!"

Indeed, it was a full moon outside, and it shone brightly. There it was amidst the stars lighting up the sky. "If it wasn't for the moon, the night would be so dark. We wouldn't be able to count the days of the month. Oh, God, forgive me! I was wrong to worship your cousin, the sun. I worship you, Mr. Moon! Thank you!"

Abram continued bowing all night along. But then… the morning came and… where did the moon go? Abram felt so sad. What if there was no God?

If God wasn't the sun, or the moon, or the stars, or the statues, what could God be?

And that's when it hit him. "Of course! God isn't the sun or the moon or the stars or the earth or the water—but each of those is part of God. There is something, a great being, who created all of this. There must be only one of these beings, and that being is God."

Indeed, Abram thus became the very first person ever to believe in one God. For this reason, God rewarded Abram, whispering a breath of "h" sound into his name. Abram thus became Abraham, the father of many nations.

Inside the Sparks

Abraham is considered the founding father of Judaism, which is the first monotheistic faith, and therefore he is also the founder of Christianity and Islam.

The present story deals with Abraham's first revelation and his confrontation with the question of a single God, God's essence and power. The book of Genesis devotes vast space to the tales of Abraham and his behavior, as well as his altercations with the residents of the land of Canaan, his values, and his worldview. The biblical text between the end of Chapter 11 and the end of Chapter 25 presents a series of stories about Abraham, who was born to Terah in Ur of the Chaldees. At the age of seventy-five, following a command from God, he leaves Haran and travels to the land of Canaan. Despite the extensive and varied information about Abraham the adult, the biblical text provides very little information about Abraham as a child and adolescent. The text does not specify what his approach and worldview were like as a child, and how his monotheistic belief came to be formed.

The present story is based on an interpretation, or "Midrash." The word Midrash refers to ancient Jewish texts that interpret various aspects of the Bible. In many cases, the Midrash includes stories, fables and legends that expand and complete the stories of the Bible. In addition to being an interesting completion of the biblical story regarding Abraham's

childhood, the present story also allows the readers to identify with the character of the spiritual leader as a child.

The story has a clear central message, which suggests that even in his childhood Abraham logically understood the existence of a single God. Despite its simplicity and its clear central message, the story may be used to develop a conversation with children. This conversation may refer to several themes at varying levels of depth, according to the child's age and the reader's willingness to elaborate the discussion. While discussing faith in one God, it is possible, depending on the children's age, to discuss our human need to understand the reasons for things that happen in our world. In religious settings, there is clearly no need to justify the importance of God and his place. Among believers, it may be important to address the standing and power of God as opposed to idols, including the sun, the moon, and the stars, and also man-made idols. Is worshipping the stars, the sun, and the moon the same as worshiping statues? It might be important to ask why Abraham believed that idol-worship was wrong.

The story is important for non-believers as well. It may be used as a basis for explaining the development of human thought and discussing the functionality of having faith, searching for meaning, and understanding the environment.

Abraham's rational approach may also be discussed with younger children. The story of Abraham demonstrates thinking deductively, drawing conclusions, and exercising judgment. Abraham tests the logic of attributing God-like powers to stars, the sun, and the moon. He extends this logic to attributing superhuman forces to man-made objects. This process of fact-finding and understanding relationships among objects and phenomena is the basis of scientific thinking. The discussion with children may be expanded to various questions pertaining to understanding the causes of various phenomena. Why is it important for us to understand the reasons for things? What is the significance of curiosity and a desire to know?

Although Abraham's behavior toward his father may be seen as a negative example of disobedience and disrespect toward a parent, his independence of thought and willingness to explore, understand, and not accept information from a single source are remarkable. It is important not to ignore the possibility that a child might conclude that Abraham did not respect his father. This is not the message that we would like to convey. The message should be that even if one disagrees with one's parents, the issue should be discussed and the circumstances explored. In a way, monotheism suggests absolute authority and willingness to obey those who have higher status. There is no reason to undermine parents' authority, and the possibly problematic example of Abraham's behavior allows a discussion of what is permitted and what is desirable in parent-child relationships. Teachers may feel more comfortable developing a discussion of this point from a neutral perspective, but parents may also use the story as a basis for a discussion in which the limits of children's appropriate behavior are pointed out, as well as a means of reaching agreement among family members.

A central dilemma of childrearing is the conflict that parents and teachers experience between the desire to instill obedience and acceptance of social rules and limitations and the intention to educate children to think independently. Observation of Abraham's behavior and his father's eventual willingness to be convinced by the arguments demonstrates a process of coping with this dilemma.

A different level of discussion, which is more abstract and appropriate for older children, departs from the literal meaning of the story and addresses its symbolic meaning. We can shift the story into the mind and see Abraham's questions and attempts to find out the truth as a process of introspection and self-examination. Examination of internal images and internal priorities is the essence of moral struggles. Who are our idols? What ideas and beliefs do not truly serve us? Is there a better, more appropriate, or more moral approach or worldview? Sometimes we have to cope with ideas that are partial or not ready, or that do not provide a complete answer to our dilemma. Only when we recognize the idols in our mind can we find a satisfactory solution. This approach encourages individuals to engage in dialogue with themselves, supports skepticism and critical thinking, and promotes examination of our existing beliefs in a logical and organized manner.

If you like, a simpler yet equally important message is our relationship to various people who influence us. We should occasionally examine our information sources and their degree of credibility. With all due respect to opinion leaders, media celebrities and politicians, who has integrity and deserves our trust, and who is merely an idol that pretends to be telling the truth about what is best for us?

It is important to give our children the means to examine the vast amount of information they receive and select only its valuable components. For example, we should teach them to consume media wisely, to identify commercial messages and propaganda, and to cross-check information to verify its credibility. Paying attention, thinking critically, and being willing to examine various sources of information are important skills that children should acquire at an early age.

Questions

1. What is the role of the sun and the moon in the story of Abraham?

2. What is the role of the statues in the store of Abraham's father?

3. Why did Abraham think that the sun and the moon could not be gods? Why did he think that the statues could not be gods?

4. How did Abraham explain the broken statues to his father? What did his explanation prove?

5. Did Abraham disrespect his father?

6. How did Abraham reach the conclusion that there is only one God? What were his thoughts before?

7. Have you ever felt that your mother or father was wrong about something? Did you say anything? What would be a respectful way to share your differing opinion?

8. What does a "sculpture" mean nowadays? How do we use sculptures in modern-day society? Why do you think people have sculptures today?

9. Why does Abraham consider idol-worship to be wrong in this story? Is it always wrong?

10. Sometimes we have different thoughts or opinions about things. How do we know what is right? How can we learn about new ideas? How can we tell if they are true or not?

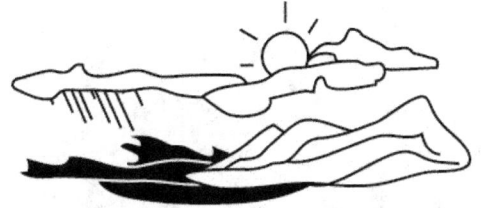

DAY FIVE: Jonah and the Great Fish
God Creates the Birds, Sea Creatures, and Insects

And God said: "Let the waters swarm with swarms of living creatures, and let fowl fly above the earth in the open firmament of heaven." And God created the great sea-monsters, and every living creature that creepeth, wherewith the waters swarmed, after its kind, and every winged fowl after its kind; and God saw that it was good. And God blessed them, saying: "Be fruitful, and multiply, and fill the waters in the seas, and let fowl multiply in the earth." And there was evening and there was morning, a fifth day. (Genesis 1:20–23)

Jonah was a special kind of person, a prophet, someone who receives important messages from God. Whenever God told Jonah to do something, he would do it (Well, wouldn't you?) because if God said so, well, it had to be right! Jonah worked hard, because there was always important work for him to take care of. There was always someone who needed a shoulder to cry on, or an animal to rescue from a dangerous situation, or an important lesson to teach.

One day, after much work, Jonah was relaxing outside. Leaning up against a tree, he thought to himself how tiring it was always to fight evil. He wanted to rest a bit, take a vacation. It was time.

At that very moment, Jonah heard a voice. Well, not just any voice, THE voice, you know which one I mean… "JOOOOOOONAH!" Yup, it was God! Jonah wanted to curl up in a ball and hide. He was just soooo tired. But of course he would do whatever God wanted, so instead he sat up straight.

"How can I be of service?" Jonah asked earnestly.

"Jonah, there are some people who really need your help."

"They do?" Jonah stood up. Now was clearly not a time to rest. There might be people who need help buying food, or finding a home, or even worse… "I will help them!"

"Wonderful," God responded. "I need you to go to the city of Nineveh. That is where the people most need you."

"What is going on there? Are they poor? Are they troubled? Are there earthquakes or hurricanes? I want to be prepared with all the right equipment!"

"You won't need any of that, Jonah. All you need is yourself. These people are not in any physical danger. But they do need help. They are behaving meanly to each other. I want you to go to them and teach them to think of other people's feelings, and to say they are sorry."

Jonah was confused. These people didn't seem to need help at all. They seemed bad. And if they were so bad, maybe they deserved to be punished. Why should he help them if they were wicked?

"I know," Jonah thought. "Maybe if I take a little vacation, maybe God won't notice. God is so busy anyway, making the world run and all. I don't want to go talk to mean people. I'll just take a little trip to Tarshish. It is far away and maybe God won't find me…."

Just then, Jonah noticed a large ship on the horizon. "Perfect!" Jonah thought, and ran to the ship. He climbed aboard and immediately found a little ladder leading to a small room downstairs. There, he fell fast asleep.

Jonah was soon awakened by a loud thump! The ship was bobbing up and down—there must be a storm outside! Jonah ran out of the room to peek outside. Sure enough, there was a terrible storm. The passengers were all huddled together, afraid… and that's when Jonah knew—it was his fault there was a terrible storm. The sea was looking for him. The people of Nineveh needed him. God had told him this, and here he was running away….

"Don't worry!" he called out. "God is looking for me. Throw me into the sea and you all will be ok." But the sailors did not want to harm Jonah, and tried to row the boat to shore. However, the sea grew rougher and rougher. Wavier and wavier!!! Finally to save themselves, they did what Jonah suggested and threw him into the water.

Down, down, down he fell, into the endless foamy water of the ocean as Jonah fell deeper and deeper still. What was happening? Was he going to drown?

Suddenly, a huge whale swam by. Before Jonah knew what hit him, the whale opened its mouth and with a big "UMMM!!" gobbled Jonah up. Jonah went sliding, sliding, sliding into the whale's tummy. "Uh, oh," thought Jonah, "I'm in trouble now!"

When Jonah woke up, he was still in the whale's stomach. "What?" gasped Jonah, "Am I still alive? How could this be?" Immediately, Jonah began to pray: "Oh, God, if you let me out of here alive, I promise I will go to Nineveh and help the people learn to say they're sorry. I promise!"

Just then, the big fish swam up and down and all around until it reached the shore. There it opened its mouth and out, with a sea full of water, came Jonah!

A voice called out to Jonah: "It is time, Jonah. You cannot run away. Will you now go to Nineveh?" Jonah knew there was no way to hide. Reluctantly, he began his journey. For three days and three nights, Jonah traveled.

He arrived to a crowd of people arguing and fighting. Jonah gathered the people together. The people started pushing and shoving each other, all trying to get closer to Jonah.

"STOP!" Jonah was finally able to shout. "I want you to hear my message. I came to you to teach you something important. Something that I also had to learn. We all know how to be nice to each other, and how important it is to say we are sorry when we're not so nice. It's not always easy, but it is the right thing to do. A whale helped me learn that—I knew I needed to come here but I tried to run away. The whale brought me back here, to you. Say you are sorry to each other, and to God, and God will forgive you and help you all be better people."

"And if we don't listen to you?" asked one of the people.

"Well," Jonah shrugged. "If you don't, God will destroy Nineveh and everyone in it."

When the people of Nineveh heard this, they became very frightened. Could he be telling the truth? One by one, they turned to each other to say they were sorry for lying or cheating or stealing or whining or taking or hiding or hitting or pushing. And one by one, they each forgave each other.

Even the King of Nineveh rose from his throne and apologized. "Everyone," the King announced. "We must not eat or drink. We need to pray together so that God can forgive us for the all the bad we have done."

And this is how Jonah – and God – saved the people of Nineveh.

Yet Jonah was still unhappy. He still did not feel that the people of Nineveh should be saved. They were wicked people. Jonah went outside the city walls in despair and sat in the heat of the baking sun. God took mercy on him and shielded him from the sun with a big leafy tree, called a "gourd." Jonah leaned against the tree and was soon fast asleep.

In his dream, God came to him. "You did good, Jonah," God whispered. "All people are my children. Today you helped a few of my children become better people. And you also learned a thing or two. I won't be happy when you run away from me, but I promise I will always be with you."

Jonah woke up feeling good. A little worm was gnawing on a leaf above him. In fact, the worm had nibbled almost the entire tree. Now, there was no longer any shade to protect Jonah from the hot sun. "Oh God!" Jonah cried out. "I thought you said you would always protect me! "

"Yes, indeed," God replied. "But you see how much you miss that single tree? So too would I miss my people—even if they did behave badly. I promised long ago, after the flood, that I would never destroy my people again. They would always have a second chance, just as you did, Noah. After all, everyone makes mistakes!"

Jonah knew that God was right, and that when it came to people making mistakes, everyone deserved a second chance. After all, Jonah had gotten one, and now it was time to forgive the people of Nineveh and anyone else who was ready to apologize and do the right thing.

Inside the Sparks

The essence of the story is this: God tells Jonah to go to warn the people of Nineveh to repent of their wickedness or they will be destroyed. Jonah does not want to do this, but does not say this to God directly. He does not say "yes" and he does not say "no" but instead runs away to Tarshish and boards ship. God pursues Jonah with a great wind to remind him of his mission. Jonah wants to die and tells the sailors to throw him overboard. However, God saves Jonah from drowning by having a great fish swallow him. Jonah prays to God from the belly of the fish, and after three days and three nights Jonah is spit out onto dry land. Jonah goes to Nineveh and again says he wants to die. This time God provides a gourd to protect Jonah from the sun. Finally, Jonah learns the lesson of mercy and forgiveness. We cannot overestimate the importance of the fact that Jonah's life is saved twice, first by a big fish and later by a gourd. Every creature and creation on this earth is important. And they all must be treated with respect.

This is a relatively simple yet profound story about a prophet who is sent on a mission by his God, and in an unusual move for the biblical text, tries to evade the mission. The story of Jonah occupied many interpreters of the Bible, who tried to understand its meaning and especially to justify Jonah's attempt to avoid warning the people of Nineveh. A number of questions arise.

Jonah is assigned what seems to be a humane mission, which may lead to the salvation of the people of Nineveh. Why does he not go? Is it simply Jonah's selfishness and unwillingness to help people in distress? It is tempting to see the people of Nineveh as people in distress needing help, and the psychological literature is filled with examples of bystander apathy. We may witness others suffering from injustice or wrongdoing, experiencing distress, making mistakes, acting imprudently, or transgressing. We do not always provide help to others, even if we can do so. Denial of help only rarely results from misunderstanding or inability to identify others' distress. Sometimes we worry that we might get hurt while providing help or that providing help would be too costly for us. In other cases, we may believe that we are unable to help or that the needy person will refuse to accept our help or to heed our advice. When in the company of other people, we may expect others to offer help and therefore refrain from doing so ourselves. Indeed, the well-known case of Kitty Genovese's murder raised awareness of circumstances in which people may refrain from helping. In 1964, Kitty Genovese was killed by a serial rapist and murderer. The murder lasted about thirty minutes and was witnessed by dozens of her neighbors, yet none of them called the police or offered to help in any way.

Researchers who attempted to understand why witnesses failed to intervene in the Kitty Genovese case, and other cases where someone was in obvious need of help, discovered that individuals usually offer help when they are alone. However, when they are part of a large group of bystanders, individuals become less likely to offer help. John Darley and Bibb Latane demonstrated this phenomenon in a laboratory study in 1968. The participants in their experiment were placed alone in a room and told that they would take part in a

discussion with others over an intercom but that their microphone would be off part of the time in order to give everyone a chance to speak. In fact, they listened to a conversation recorded in advance, in which one of the participants pretended to have a seizure at some point. The findings showed that the more people the participants believed to be present, the less likely they were to offer help and the longer they waited before seeking help. The explanation that was offered for these findings, known as diffusion of responsibility, suggests that when others are present, people assume that someone else is going to help and therefore refrain from doing so themselves.

However, as interesting as this data is, is it really applicable to Jonah's dilemma? If so, in what ways? After all, the people of Nineveh were probably more like the victimizer than the victim. They were more like the man who assaulted Kitty Genovese than like Kitty Genovese herself. Shouldn't that man have been stopped, even if it meant injuring or killing him? Is the wrong-doer no different than the victim?

The people of Nineveh are probably not much different than the people of Sodom and Gomorrah. So the question emerges: Why does God ask Jonah to help them when previously he had argued with Abraham over whether the people of Sodom should be saved? Another question is why Jonah does not answer God directly, either accepting or rejecting his assignment, but instead runs away. A third question is why Jonah wants to die after running away, and why God saves his life. A fourth question is the importance of the role of God's creations, first the fish, and then the gourd, in saving Jonah's life. And the final question is, how does God tries to teach Jonah the notion of forgiveness and the awareness that people can change?

One may use the story of Jonah in order to facilitate an extended discussion of the human need to give and receive help. How might we increase the likelihood of helping? With older children, the issue of bystander intervention and the meaning of diffusion of responsibility may also be discussed. These are important issues to address in order to promote pro-social behavior.

The story of Jonah contains additional themes that are relevant to the issue of helping. The mariners on the ship struggle with the storm, and even when they realize that Jonah is the cause of God's wrath, they do not rush to judgment. This is a message that is worthy of elaboration. In situations of stress, and occasionally in other times, groups of children or adults tend to look for scapegoats on which they can take out their anger and aggression. The conduct of the mariners and the dilemmas they experience regarding Jonah's treatment may serve as a basis for a discussion of relationships between individuals and groups and treatment of minorities and those who are different. In a gesture of self-sacrifice, Jonah suggests that the mariners cast him into the sea, because he does not want them to perish due to his sin. This scene may be used to facilitate a discussion of self-sacrifice and the importance of accepting responsibility for one's deeds.

An additional theme appears in the story of Jonah's salvation. Although Jonah is punished for disobeying God, his punisher appears to be patient and compassionate. The prophet prays in the belly of the fish, praises God, and asks for God's forgiveness. God forgives and reveals one of the important themes of the story—forgiveness of sin and absolution. The residents of Nineveh take Jonah's warning and reprimand seriously, see the threat of punishment as a binding message, and therefore repent and mend their ways. God sees that they have indeed mended their ways and forgives them. The topic of warning, remorse, and behavior improvement is very important in an educational context. It is a salient issue in relationships between parents and children and between teachers and students.

In many families, parents may become upset due to their children's negative deeds or omissions. Punishment should be limited and controlled, and most importantly, allow for a possibility of behavior improvement. The motivation for behavior improvement increases if the child believes in the seriousness of the punishment but also in the possibility of avoiding it by seeking forgiveness and improving future behavior. Parents sometimes find it difficult to communicate that their anger and the resulting punishment do not indicate that they have stopped loving their child. They may not approve of the deed, but they still love the doer. A discussion of this topic may explore children's reactions to threats and punishments and clarify issues of punishment, forgiveness, and atonement. God realizes that Jonah is not convinced that the people of Nineveh should be spared, and uses an allegory to elucidate His message. He compares Jonah's pain over the loss of the gourd to the loss of the great city of Nineveh and its many residents. God reprimands

Jonah for his narrow egotistical view. He grieves the withered gourd but does not have compassion for the people of Nineveh and is not willing to give them the benefit of the doubt and a chance to make amends.

As humans, we are sensitive to our own losses and sorrows. But what about the suffering of others? Members of human societies must be considerate and compassionate toward others, and not confine themselves to an egocentric approach. It is important to begin to develop the social skill of empathy at a young age. One must be aware of others' points of view and be sensitive to their pain. The issue of consideration toward others, understanding their distress, and attempting to assist them is an essential foundation in every educational stage. In the absence of this foundation, social adaptation and the formation of a functional society become very difficult.

A possible explanation for Jonah's attempt to avoid helping the people of Nineveh is his pessimism about his ability to convince them to mend their ways. Several interpreters suggested that Jonah saw the people of Nineveh as irredeemable offenders and therefore did not believe that they might change. Perhaps Jonah was afraid of being corrupted by their ways, like Lot and his family were corrupted by the ways of Sodom. There God is portrayed as insisting that Lot and his family separate from the Sodomites, despairing of any chance of changing them. When Lot's wife looks back, in fact, she

is turned into a pillar of salt. Why does God act differently here? Are the people of Nineveh different than the people of Sodom, or has God changed? God's insistence that Jonah warn the people of Nineveh, and Jonah's eventual success, emphasize an additional point: even if something seems impossible to change and possibly hopeless, we must persist, not give up, and try to remain optimistic for as long as possible. Persistence, determination, and minimization of pessimism characterize those who cope successfully and eventually reach their goals. Yet why does Jonah want to die after his success? Does he feel that sparing the wicked people of Nineveh is unjust? Is it unjust to forgive a criminal? Should the criminal not be punished? How do we integrate justice and mercy?

Questions

1. How does the story of Jonah begin? What was Jonah trying to avoid? Why did he not directly accept or reject his assignment to go to Nineveh, but run away to Tarshish?

2. What happened to Jonah on the way to Tarshish? Why did it happen?

3. Why did Jonah suggest that the mariners cast him into the sea?

4. Why is Jonah's life saved by a fish? What does this mean with regard to how we should treat animals? How should children treat their pets? Why should we water plants?

5. What did God want from the people of Nineveh? Why did God eventually forgive them?

6. Over what did Jonah feel compassion? What can we learn from the story of the gourd?

7. When should we forgive someone who behaved badly? What does forgiveness mean? Does it mean the wrongdoer is not accountable for his actions? Should he not be punished? Where does justice enter into the equation?

8. What makes a child behave badly? What can the parents do to punish the action without rejecting the child? How should the child react?

Questions

9. Have you ever felt like you wanted to run away from something you had to do? How did you handle this?

10. Why is it important to persevere and make efforts in order to achieve something and not give in prematurely? Why is it important to have hope that people and events can change?

DAY SIX: Adam Names the Animals
God Gives Man Dominion over All Other Living Creatures

And God said: "Let the earth bring forth the living creature after its kind, cattle, and creeping thing, and beast of the earth after its kind." And it was so. And God made the beast of the earth after its kind, and the cattle after their kind, and every thing that creepeth upon the ground after its kind; and God saw that it was good. And God said: "Let us make man in our image, after our likeness; and let them have dominion over the fish of the sea, and over the fowl of the air, and over the cattle, and over all the earth, and over every creeping thing that creepeth upon the earth." And God created man in His own image, in the image of God created He them. And God blessed them; and God said unto them: "Be fruitful, and multiply, and replenish the earth, and subdue it; and have dominion over the fish of the sea, and over the fowl of the air, and over every living thing that creepeth upon the earth." And God said: "Behold, I have given you every herb yielding seed, which is upon the face of all the earth, and every tree, in which there is the fruit of a tree yielding seed—to you it shall be for food; and to every fowl of the air, and to every thing that creepeth upon the earth, wherein there is a living soul, (I have given) every green herb for food." And it was so. And God saw every thingthat He had made, and behold, it was very good. And there was evening and there was morning, the sixth day.   (Genesis 1:24–31)

After the earth was created, with the trees and the seas and the skies, God sprinkled the seas with fish and whales and dolphins and sharks. God zapped the skies with birds and butterflies and bees and flies.

Then, like a great artist, God breathed a sigh. God gathered the angels and whispered to them: "It is good. It is good. I did good."

"Oh yes," they agreed. "You did great!"

"Great…? Mmmm…" God wasn't quite satisfied. The world still seemed quite empty. On the ground itself there were no living things, other than flowers, plants, and trees. It looked beautiful, magical, a garden, "a masterpiece!" as the angels seemed to think. But God wasn't quite so sure. So God created animals of all types to inhabit the earth. Yet it still seemed somehow… lonely.

"If only there was one of us down there," God sighed to the angels. "It would be so nice to have a friend down there, someone maybe to talk to." God looked around at his angels, who always flew by his side. Whatever God asked for they would always agree to do.

"Whatever you wish will be done," they smiled and nodded.

"Hmmm…. Perhaps someone not quite so… agreeable. Maybe even someone who would argue sometimes. Nah! Who would dare argue with me? Wait!" God exclaimed. "I have it! Let's make an image down below. This image will be much like us, but more like a shadow of us down on earth." The angels all nodded in agreement. "My goodness, the creator was so smart! Who knew what God would think of next?" They whispered and they nodded with a smile and a wink.

Just then a great wind swooped down. It collected the dust of the earth. Almost like a tornado, the dust began to form rapidly into a cone. The birds continued to fly above and the fish continued to swim. Unbeknownst to them God was creating again! Soon, the tornado-like cone of dust began to form arms, began to form legs. There stood a figure made out of dust, shaped out of clay. "This figure will be called 'Adam,' which in Hebrew means both earth and man," God announced, and he will be made in our image. With that, God whispered a breath of life into Adam's nostrils.

Adam immediately opened his eyes.

God looked down with satisfaction. And together the angels "oooooh!"ed and "ahhhh"ed! "You have outdone yourself!" they whispered with an awe-inspired smile. "Unbelievable!"

But God wasn't quite happy, looking down at the lonely creature down below. "How can I make just one like him?" God asked the angels. "He will feel so lonesome on his own."

"Wait, I have it!" God proclaimed. "I will find him a helpmeet, someone to be by his side, a friend!"

And with a poof, the string of animals that God had created gathered around Adam. "Adam," God commanded. "Choose. Look at each of these, name them one by one. And tell me when you find the one for you."

Wide-eyed, the newly born Adam curiously examined the creatures all around. Which one would be the one for him?

A tiny little one crawled onto his foot, tickling his toe. Adam giggled. "You! What are you, little thing?" he leaned to examine. A little red bug sat on his big toe. "Are you the partner for me?" Adam asked. "Maybe… Your colors are so beautiful. Your shape is quite angelic. Speak to me." He leaned over to touch her, but off she flew, with red and black tiny little wings. "Ah!" he sighed. "So magical! A lady-bug you are. I call you 'lady bug.' Lovely, but not the one for me."

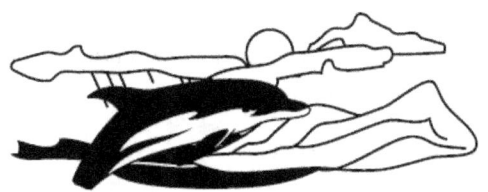

Adam wasn't worried. There were so many to choose from. And each was coming to him for its name. "Wow, a big strong one. Perhaps you will be the one. Large and beautiful. Heavy as can be. Relaxed, bathing there in the muddy swamp. Can I get nearer to you?" A big splash splashed his back. "Oh. Maybe not. I'll call you 'hippopotamus'—'hippo' for short. You are hip, but 'oh!' not quite for me."

Just then a tunnel of earth erupted right next to his feet. An animal arose straight from the earth. "Just from the ground—wow. But I don't think I want to live down there, so you I will call 'ground hog.' Yes, that will be your name."

And on the edge of the earth that was dug up, a clear and slimy creature slithered past. "Are you worming your way away from me? Hmmm… an 'earth worm.'"

Big ferocious animals leaped into his sight: animals he named a "leopard" (for his leaping) or "tigrrrrrrrrrrrrrrrrrrrrrrs!" and "bearrrrrrrrrrrrrrrrrrrrrs" (for their "GRRRRR!").

"Lizzzzzzzzzzards" and "Sssssssssssnakes" ssssslithered away from him. Grasshoppers hopped in the grass. Bees buzzed. Horses sounded hoarse when they "neighghgh"ed. And those monkeys sure monkeyed around!

All of them were magical and beautiful and interesting. But none of them felt particularly pleasant to talk to or even to hug. Even the cute little animals, such as the puppies that he petted or the kittens that he'd catch, were soft and cuddly but didn't quite feel right.

One by one, Adam named all the animals. One by one, each animal received its name. Adam stood alone. Happy and contented. So many wonderful friends in one day!

But still—he felt a bit empty. A quiet. Each animal scurried off with its friends while Adam stood behind—alone.

"Hush," God whispered to the angels. "My work is not yet done, you see. Sit silently, and just watch me." Immediately a great silence fell upon the heavens as the angels eagerly watched what their master would do next.

Though the sun was still brightly shining, and night had fallen in the sky, God sent a sleepy breeze over Adam's eyes. "Oh," Adam sighed. "A long day. Maybe I'll take a little nap."

And with that Adam curled up next to a tree and slept. "Shhhhh...." God whispered. "A deep sleep for you. We have a little operation here to do. Scalpel!" God announced, and the angel soon appeared. Before Adam knew it a rib had been removed. "Aha!" God proclaimed. "The best surgeon around!"

"Wow!" the angels marveled in agreement at the wonders of their God.

"And now!" God began. "It is time to make your match." God took the rib and formed it piece by piece. First, the trunk, then the head, the arms, the legs, the face, the hair. And with a poof, Adam awoke.

There, standing before him, was the loveliest creature he'd ever seen. She stood on two legs just as he did. She looked so much like him, but far more beautiful. "You," he began. "You will… oh!" Adam felt a pang in his rib. At that moment he understood.

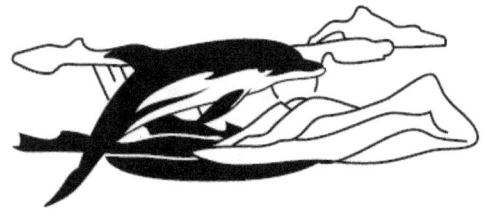

"I am man. You must be wo–man. You came out of my flesh, out of my bones. You I will call 'Eve' for it is you who will be the mother of my children, the mother of all living things. You're the one. My mate! My partner! My wife."

Adam took Eve's hand and introduced her to the animals that he had named, one by one. "This is our garden," Adam explained. "This is our home. Each of the animals is our friend. God asked that I name them and we must take care of them. Will you help me?"

"Of course," Eve smiled. "I am your helpmeet. I will help you and you will help me. We will never be afraid to express our own opinions to each other. We are of the same flesh. We are family. We will take care of all the animals that you have named. It is our special responsibility."

Adam reached over to Eve. The two of them hugged. It was beautiful. Holding each other felt like two missing puzzle pieces finally fitting together.

God and the angels peered down. "Truly magnificent!" the angels all exclaimed.

And God had to admit. "I really am quite good."

An entire world had been created. And a match for Adam had finally been found. Now, God's work was done. It was time for the heavens to rest.

Inside the Sparks

The story of Adam naming the animals illustrates the theme of the sixth day of creation. On this sixth day, God creates the land animals and human beings (male and female), the human beings alone in the likeness of God, and gives human beings dominion over all other living creatures that God has created. (Genesis 1:24–28). God has created the animals, and they are important. This sense of dominion is not a license for the human being to destroy or humiliate but implies a responsibility of the human being to care for God's creatures. Since only human beings are created in God's image, human beings have a unique responsibility to care for animals.

The sense of responsibility is amplified in verses 18–20 in Genesis 2, when Adam names the animals.

The first man essentially engages in primeval fundamental scientific activity: He classifies and categorizes the animal world, and effectively defines it for the next generations. This is an important activity in the intellectual experience of every human being. Perceiving and understanding the world necessitate order, structure, and labeling of the objects that surround us. It is the human way of perceiving the world and making it more comprehensible.

In a way, this activity extends the act of Creation, which involved setting boundaries between water and heavens and between water and land. Adam as God's emissary participates in the organization of chaos, sets boundaries, and establishes order and regularity.

As God's emissary, Adam does not set up a random order. He defines identities. The names given to the animals distinguish them from each other and provide separation and individuation. At the literal level, Adam appears to engage in the organization and ordering of the world around him, but this activity may be seen as a metaphor for internal order and organization, which involve defining what belongs where, who is different from whom, and where the boundaries of the self begin and end. What about my dependence on my parents? To what extent am I separate from my parents, and do I have an individual essence of my own? What about defining my own identity? What is the meaning of naming? Who gave me my name? What does my name symbolize? Did my parents intend for my name to mean something? To what extent am I content with my name?

There is yet another function of naming something. The namer assumes a responsibility for that which he has named. God assigns a mission to Adam: to give the recently created animals and birds appropriate names. It appears that the assignment of this role to Adam, even though the Creator could have carried it out by himself, represents God's intention to give humans dominion over the animal kingdom, which implies that humans have a responsibility to care for the animal world. The biblical text clarifies the responsibility of humans uniquely made in God's image to care over animals. It also emphasizes the command to be considerate toward animals, not to cause them unnecessary suffering, and to treat them as creatures of Creation, equally worthy of respect and admiration. We have already seen the importance of the animal world and discussed other aspects of the treatment of animals in the story of Noah.

This story, which chronologically appears before the story of Noah in the biblical text, provides an opportunity to discuss ecology and the manner in which we as humans treat the wildlife around us. In the past, humans may have taken God's message on the sixth day of creation literally: "'… and have dominion over the fish of the sea, and over the fowl of the air, and over every living thing that creepeth upon the earth'" (Genesis 1:28). Nowadays, we understand that ruling the animal world does not mean that we should be cruel to animals, and certainly not hurt them or extinguish them.

Adam's act of naming the animals establishes his dominion over them, but he must realize that with dominion comes responsibility. God gives Adam resources, but these are limited and must be handled carefully and considerately. It is important to understand that if humans do not nurture and protect wildlife and plant-life and exploit them irresponsibly, they will eventually instigate a serious ecological disaster that would be damaging to their welfare.

The discussion may be expanded from ecological issues and the need to be considerate toward animals to the need to be considerate toward other humans, whoever they may be. One may address questions of personal identity. How are humans similar to each other and how are they different? It should be emphasized that despite our need to establish a clearly defined identity and despite individual differences between persons, all humans are equal and we should not hurt others or neglect those who are weaker than we are and dependent on us.

Why do we need to name animals and persons? Did we have a chance to suggest a name for another child—a sibling or a relative? What about naming pets, dolls, or toys that do not portray humans or animals? I can give a doll the name of my choice because it is my doll. I might get suggestions from others, but I make the final choice about naming those that I own or that are under my charge.

Another important theme appears in the first verse: "It is not good that the man should be alone; I will make a helpmeet for him." Several interpreters of the Bible addressed this verse in various contexts. We would like to focus on the social message that this verse conveys literally, which emphasizes the importance of social relations. Humans are creatures that need companionship, and therefore children should acquire social skills from an early age. The fundamental skills have already been mentioned above and in reference to other stories: patience, tolerance, consideration, and flexibility. One must devote efforts to developing friendships and engage in equitable relationships. Good friendship is a source of joy as well as confidence and security. This appears to be one of the most important messages conveyed by the biblical story. One of the most important roles of parents and teachers is to educate children to form and maintain social relationships with other children around them. This educational process may benefit from discussions of the behaviors of biblical and literary characters, which have implications for social relations.

A final note on being alone: Despite the above discussion, the ability to cope on one's own may be considered a virtue in certain cases. Being alone does not necessarily entail loneliness. The ability to take time off to be alone and to enjoy doing or thinking about things on one's own may be beneficial and not always problematic.

Questions

1. Why are human beings alone created in God's image?
   What does this mean in terms of responsibility to the animals?

2. Why did God assign the role of naming the animals to Adam?

3. Why is it important to give different names to the animals?
   Why is it important that every person have his own name?

4. How did you get your name? Does your name have a meaning?
   Were you named after someone in your family or in history?

5. How do you think that someone who names a person or an animal feels? Have you ever named a pet?
   What made you give it its particular name? Did it fit?

6. What are the advantages that humans have over animals?

7. Why is it important to prevent cruelty to animals?

8. Let us talk about the importance of various animals to humans.
   Can you give some examples of ways animals help humans?

9. What is the importance of nature reserves and laws that prohibit fishing or hunting in certain areas?

10. Why is it not good that man should be alone?
    What are the benefits and drawbacks of being with others?

DAY SEVEN: The Sabbath
God Rests on the Sabbath and Human Beings Need to Rest Also
The Prophet Elijah Rests and Recovers His Strength

And the heaven and the earth were finished, and all the host of them. And on the seventh day God finished His work which He had made; and He rested on the seventh day from all His work which He had made. And God blessed the seventh day, and hallowed it; because in it He rested from all His work which God in creating had made. (Genesis 2:1–3)

A long time ago, in Shomron, King Ahab and Queen Jezebel ruled over the land. For a long time, the Hebrews believed in one God, whereas their neighbors believed in many gods, with the chief of the gods being Ba'al, god of nature. Queen Jezebel wanted everyone to worship her god, Ba'al, and the gods of nature. So, she ordered all of God's prophets to be destroyed, and only Ba'al's prophets to remain.

So it was that many Hebrew prophets were killed. Only one managed to escape Queen Jezebel's wrath. His name was Elijah, which means "God is my God" Or "my God is The God." As a prophet, Elijah was one of the very few people in history who could actually speak to God. In one of these conversations, God instructed Elijah to help a widow in Tzarfat. Elijah showed great kindness to the woman and to her son who had been starving. With the help of God, Elijah arranged for the woman to have enough food to survive. Later, Elijah prayed to God to restore the life of the widow's son who had suddenly taken ill.

Not long after, Elijah learned that God was going to punish the Hebrews for turning away from God. "Everyone, God has decreed that there will be a great famine in the land. Only once you return to God will it rain again, allowing for food to grow and water to be plentiful again."

Everyone ignored Elijah, since they didn't believe in his god. But Elijah was right. There was no rain for three full years. Everyone was thirsty. Even the plants and trees were thirsty—and so no food grew. People were hungry. More than anything, they wanted some rain. After three years of famine, God appeared to Elijah and said: "You must show the people that I am the only God. Once you do so I will bring rain upon the land again and people will be able to eat and drink freely." Elijah was excited—rain again? This is wonderful news. All he would have to do now was to convince the people to believe in God. And since God's decree about the famine came true, wouldn't they all easily believe?

"Hmm…" thought Elijah. "Maybe I can convince the Queen first. If she takes on God as her god, surely the people will follow!" Immediately, Elijah sent a notice to the queen, asking to meet with her.

But as fast as he could blink, Elijah's note from the queen returned. He scanned the message to see how soon she would see him. Unfortunately, this was not the message Queen Jezebel had sent. Instead, she replied that she refused to see him. After all, Elijah was not a believer in her god.

This angered Elijah. What more could he do to prove God's wisdom? "That's it!" Elijah thought to himself. "I have no choice but to challenge God's non-believers. If I don't, the rain will never come and none of us will survive!" Elijah knew what to do: "Spread the word to all of Ba'al's prophets. I would like to challenge them. We shall soon see whose god is the real God."

Everyone was curious to see what Elijah would do. How can anyone prove a god's existence? God does what God wants, not what people tell God to do! Soon, 450 prophets gathered together to show Elijah that his task was impossible. "I realize all of you have doubt," Elijah announced. "Who is the true God? Is it Ba'al the lord of the idols, or is it God, creator of the world? You may be looking for a sign, for an answer. Well, I've brought you here to make it very clear. Today before your very eyes you'll finally see the truth. Come, pay attention. Watch!!!"

"There are 450 prophets of Ba'al. There is only one prophet left for God and that is me. So I challenge all you prophets of Ba'al to a test. Prepare an altar for your god. Prepare everything but don't light the fire. When all is ready, pray to your god and ask Ba'al to light the fire so that the sacrifice will go up to the heavens in flames. If you are able to do so, we will all know that your god is the true god. If not, we will know that you and he are false. Now go!"

Immediately, the prophets began to pray. They prayed and prayed and prayed some more. "O Ba'al hear us!" they cried quietly.

"Why are you whispering?" Elijah mocked. "Call out your prayers in a loud strong voice. Do not be shy! Who knows? Perhaps your god is sleeping. Maybe he's hard of hearing. You think he could be on vacation? He may be far, so don't be shy. Pray out loud! Go on, yell!"

This they did. They called louder and louder still, but not one of the 450 prophets was able to make a fire appear to take their sacrifice up to heaven.

"Now watch." Elijah spoke. "Come close and gather round." The people did. They gathered round to watch closely what he was to do. He prepared the altar with stones all around. He dug a ditch around the altar and asked the people to fill the ditch full of water. This they did once, twice, three times as Elijah requested of them. As they filled it with water, they whispered to themselves: "How can anyone light a fire when the ditch is full of water? Surely the water would put out any flame?" But, they did as they were told, shaking their heads the entire time.

Just as evening fell, Elijah began his prayer: "Oh God, God of Abraham, Isaac, and Jacob, God of the people of Israel. I have done all that you asked of me and prepared this sacrifice for you as you requested. Hear my prayer, take my offering, so that all the people here will open their hearts to you once more."

Almost instantly, a great fire lit up the entire ditch. The fire ate up all the water before everybody's eyes. The sacrifice was burnt up into heaven as if by magic—or, more likely, by the hand of God.

Immediately, the people of Israel fell to their knees. Their hearts opened. Elijah was right, they were all one! There was only one God. And that was Adonai.

"Adonai, He is God. Adonai, He is God. Adonai, He is God!" they chanted together. "There is only one God on the earth. God connects all beings. We are all one from the same source."

"Aha!" Elijah exclaimed. "I hear something. Yes, it is the rumbling of rain. Because you have opened your hearts to God it will soon rain again. Very soon we will be able to eat and drink just as we used to!"

Though the people heard nothing, they trusted Elijah, and sure enough soon the rain poured down. It was a wonderful day for them, a true delight, for now they would eat and drink freely again. Everybody celebrated, except of course for the prophets of Ba'al. The people were so angry at the false prophets for lying to them that the prophets had no choice but to flee.

"Stop them!" the people cried out. "Kill them before they lie to anyone else!"

Elijah and his followers instantly ran after the prophets and did not return until every last one of these false prophets was slain. "Finally," Elijah thought, "Queen Jezebel will see that I am a true prophet, as were all those that had been slain so long ago. I am the only one left. And now she can finally see that I am true, and that God is the one and only God!"

Elijah sent a messenger to the queen, telling her all that had happened. Almost immediately, the messenger returned with a letter from Queen Jezebel.

"Ah!" thought Elijah. "She could not wait to reward me! Let me tear open the letter and find my great reward!" Elijah quickly opened the message and began to read.

"Dear Elijah," Queen Jezebel had begun. "I see that much has happened in recent hours. I would like to see you tomorrow afternoon."

"Oh my!" Elijah thought. "She finally wants to see me! The Queen! Wow! I have finally proven myself to her! She finally knows how truthful I really am!"

Elijah kept on reading. "I appreciate the detail with which you relayed to me all that happened to Ba'al's prophets. Tomorrow when I see you, I'll make sure the very same thing happens to you."

"Huh?" Elijah was puzzled. "The very same thing that happened to them? Happen to me? But that means — Ack! She wants to have me killed!!!"

There was no time to waste. Elijah had to flee for his life! Immediately, he began to run. He ran and he ran and he ran. He ran so far that he reached the end of town. There amidst an archway of trees was a path leading to a long winding uninhabited forest. Elijah ducked in between the trees and continued to run into the abyss. "Perhaps here I can just disappear into the wilderness," Elijah thought. His run soon slowed into a trot, and then to a leisurely walk as the only sounds around him were the crickets of the night. Soon, the sun began to set, and Elijah knew there was nowhere more to run. He would have to stop and stay the night.

Elijah collapsed under a nearby broom tree. "God of our ancestors!" Elijah called out. "I give up! I have tried as hard as I could! I have risked my life again and again – but to what purpose? The Queen not only refuses to believe in you – she wants to have me killed! Well, that's fine with me. I have lost my will to live. A person can only do so much." Elijah sighed. "I am through. Through trying to prove myself to people who couldn't care less. If it is my fate to die, let me die. I'll die right here. Under this tree. After all, what I have really done in this world that my ancestors did not do better before me? Take me, God. Let me just disappear. Right here. Right now."

With a heavy sigh, Elijah fell into a deep, exhausted sleep. He slept and slept. Here, within the silence, Elijah could find peace. Here, his mind could stop. His body could stop. Amidst the trees and the animals, he would find his way back to the very earth from which he came.

It was in this peaceful space that an angel tapped Elijah. Awakening from the long deep sleep, Elijah's eyes heavily blinked open.

"Arise, Elijah, wake up. Eat." There, before Elijah, a white tablecloth floated. On it appeared a full pitcher of water and a scrumptious-looking cake. As if in a dream, Elijah picked up a fork and began to nibble at the cake. Bit by bit Elijah ate, until the entire cake was gone.

Then, in a single breath, Elijah swallowed and lay back down to sleep. Days passed—or hours—Elijah was not sure which, when the angel tapped him once again. "Arise and eat, Elijah. Come see all I have prepared for you. Eat, enjoy and gather strength. A long journey awaits you."

Elijah arose and ate a second time. This time he regained some of his strength. He arose and began to walk. He walked forty days and forty nights until finally he arrived at Mount Horeb, the mountain of God.

As he neared the foot of the mountain, a great wind resounded across the mountain. It was strong and heavy, and Elijah could barely keep from being blown away in it. Mountains shook and rocks crumbled, but Elijah remained there at the foot of the mountain, his faith unshaken. Somehow, he knew that this wind was not of God.

Just then, the earth began to rumble. It rumbled cracked and quaked. Elijah nearly fell into one of the cracks, but he remained fearless, at the foot of God's mountain. "God is not in this earthquake," he said to himself. "God was not in the wind. God was not in the rocks. God….? Are you there…?"

Suddenly the wind stopped, and the earth grew silent. Then, it arose: a still, small voice, barely louder than a whisper. It spoke simply and clearly to Elijah: "Elijah, what is it you seek here?"

"Oh God," Elijah pleaded. "I am not sure I have the strength to fight for you anymore! The children of Israel have rejected you time and time again. They have destroyed all your other prophets, and only I remain. I have proven your power, yet still they seek my life. I have nowhere else to turn!"

"Elijah," God replied in a sweet soothing voice. "I will give you the strength. Now that you have rested, eaten, slept, and now that you have regained your strengt,h you are ready to hear My voice within you. You will not find my voice in the rumbling of the earth, or the screeching of the wind, but only in the deepest quiet. So it is with my people. Running or fighting won't bring out your strength. There is a place for that. But only when it is balanced by stillness and regeneration. Elijah, you have rested, and you have found me in the quiet. I am with you. Now, go back, share your silent strength and show the people you are not afraid to defend your God."

This Elijah did. He returned to the land and fought for justice. When Queen Jezebel ordered a man to be killed so that her husband Ahab could take over his vineyard, the prophet rushed to protest her unfair behavior. Elijah then announced the power of God to do the right thing and to save him and all of God's believers. It was in that moment, before everyone's eyes, that God sent a chariot of fire to take Elijah up to the highest of heavens, where he resides to this very day.

It is this same chariot that Elijah rides every Passover, when he comes to visit the people of Israel and give them strength during their big meal, just as the angel did for him. Elijah's deep faith and inner journey also led him to be a symbol of kindness to others. One never knows when a good deed might just be rewarded by Elijah the prophet, who may be lurking nearby. It is also said, that one day, when the people in the world are ready to be kind, peaceful and open-hearted, the great Messiah will come to bring peace on the Earth. The Messiah will be accompanied by none other than Elijah, the symbol of faith, rest, and rebirth.

Inside the Sparks

The Sabbath day is devoted to rest, renewal of strength, assessment of the situation, and self-examination. In this context, we present the story of Elijah the prophet, in which Elijah is forced to rest because all his activities make him feel exhausted and wear out his strength. Elijah needs rest in order to gather his strength and prepare for his next missions. We begin our discussion with this short snippet of Elijah's life. We discuss additional messages of his story later on.

After Elijah kills many of the prophets of Ba'al, Queen Jezebel threatens to kill him, leading Elijah to flee to the desert. Elijah arrives with his strength depleted and wishing to die. We witness the devout prophet in a moment of weakness and despair. This segment of the story may be used to facilitate a discussion of the difficulty of standing up for one's self and struggling against a persistent opponent. At times of crisis, we may feel unable to face the difficulties and demands, especially if the stressful situation persists for a long time. The human organism is capable of effortful endeavors, and ideological commitment enhances one's capabilities, but it is a limited resource that may eventually become depleted after a prolonged struggle.

This section of the story includes several lessons that should be elaborated upon and emphasized. These lessons can facilitate effective coping in situations of difficulty and crisis. Beginning with the physiological aspect, food and drink must be available for an organism to function. Although endurance and motivation can delay the gratification of basic needs, there is a limit to one's ability to cope, and attention must be paid to ensure that this limit is not crossed. In times of exhaustion, one's mental strengths are depleted as well, and one is in danger of collapsing and surrendering. Surrendering due to despair is one of the most trying human experiences. It results from an experience of helplessness and a belief that there is no way out of the situation except death. It is important to convey to children from a very young age that as long as one is alive, one must continue to strive to live one's life fully, facing whatever challenges arise. We suggest adopting the slogan "There will always be an opportunity to give in," which implies a conscious deference to the option to give in in the midst of a creative search for alternative solutions. Things change, and a situation that seems hopeless at one point, may not seem so at a later point.

In the story, the prophet receives help from a divine being who provides him with food and assistance. Empowered by his respite and the nurturing he received, Elijah gains a new perspective on his life. He abandons his despair and sets out on his journey, filled with courage and optimism. Just as divine intervention pointed Elijah to rest, people can also acknowledge for themselves the importance of taking time off in situations that are stressful and exhausting. The break and rest allows individuals to contemplate and reexamine their situation, possibly from new and different perspectives. Eventually, this will enable them to gather their strength and return to more efficient coping.

The story of Elijah the prophet presents complex dilemmas. Aside from being an interesting story, rich in miraculous acts and events that may appeal to younger children, some of the tales of the prophet represent difficult situations that are more appropriate for discussion with older children. Elijah the prophet may be seen as someone who helps people in distress. Saving the life of the widow's son is a good example that can be used in order to facilitate a conversation about a topic we discussed previously: helping others and being empathetic to their suffering. One may also discuss the prophet's ability to perform miracles. The miracles that the prophet performs provide evidence to the backing that he receives from God. When he confronts the false prophets, he uses miracles and omens in order to prove the greatness of the one true God. God is the one who heals the sick and is able to set fire to the offering, even when it is soaked with water. With younger children, one may wish to keep the discussion close to the biblical story. One can focus on Elijah's faith in one God over many and the power he gathered in this belief. One can also focus on the importance of rest and rejuvenation. With older children, it may be possible to elaborate on issues such as devotion to an idea, the need to struggle against numerous powerful opponents, and the possibility of withstanding them through the power of one's faith.

However, one may also wish to address the more problematic aspects of the story and allow children to respond to other sides of the prophet's character. Elijah may be seen as a man of great faith or a moral zealot who attacks others for their lack of faith. Elijah emphasizes his zealousness and his uncompromising view of himself as God's representative by announcing his disapproval of those who challenge God.

In a way, this approach is compatible with the moral judgment of young children. Young children's moral approach is inflexible. They tend to see the world in black and white and seek absolute justice. This is certainly a problematic approach for parents and educators, who wish to emphasize the importance of looking at an issue from several perspectives and to instill tolerance and openness. One may elaborate on the confrontation between Elijah and God, who appears to be less of an extreme zealot than his disciple Elijah.

Due to these and other difficulties in clarifying the biblical messages, the version of the story presented here is toned down and does not include the details of the violence that can be found in the original story. However, there are additional positive aspects to the prophet's character that are worthy of elaboration and may be used in order to instill values.

The prophet is devoted to maintaining justice and moral values. He does not hesitate to confront the royal authorities and to preach against social injustice. He is even willing to risk his life and to sacrifice his personal comfort in his pursuit of justice. When Queen Jezebel causes the death of Naboth so that her husband Ahab can take possession of Naboth's vineyard, the prophet rushes to protest the injustice. The expression "Hast thou killed, and also taken possessions?" has become a universal concept, which implies that those in the position of

authority do not have the right to commit crimes or injustices. This is an important educational message, which emphasizes the equality of all citizens, so that even those who hold important positions and are well respected are not allowed to do wrong by others. The power of the leader must be used for the benefit of the people and not for the leader's own benefit at the expense of the people. This is an important message that may be discussed with children of various ages, although the level of discussion must be adapted to the children's developmental stage and their level of understanding.

Questions

1. Why does the prophet Elijah wish to die?
2. Tell us what Elijah did to help others.
3. Elijah the prophet is a committed and uncompromising person. Explain these characteristics. Are they good or bad to have?
4. Why is it important to rest after a great effort? And what is the importance of the Sabbath as a weekly day of rest?
5. Have you ever worked very hard at something and needed some rest? How did you feel after you rested?
6. What do you think makes people experience despair?
7. Have you ever experienced despair? What brought on this feeling?
8. Why is it important not to give up? What can we do in order to overcome despair? How does rest help Elijah overcome despair?
9. Why is it important to help others?
10. What is injustice? What should one do when one encounters injustice?

Conclusions

The stories in this book were written for children. The book divides a child's week into a step-by-step week of creation as described in the first book of the Bible, *Genesis* or *The Beginning*. In this book we tell seven stories of biblical men to illustrate each of these days. On the first day of creation, God brings forth form from formlessness like a potter. He then divides day from night (Genesis 1:1–5). We have told the story of David and Goliath to illustrate this theme. Goliath, a walking giant, is basically a bully without form, and thus he is clumsy, awkward, and inflexible. His movements are rigid and stereotyped, and his thinking is equally stagnant. David, in comparison, is agile. His movements are supple and his thinking is creative. Note how he has used a slingshot to counter Goliath's superior strength. David runs at Goliath and throws the slingshot at him. He turns Goliath's bulk against him. Something big may appear frightening, but often bigness per se is empty. Bulk often disguises lack of definition. A formed person like David is far more flexible. He is able to dance around Goliath. So it is that form can dance around chaos. This is a very valuable lesson for a child to learn.

On the second day of creation, God separates the waters above (Heaven) from the waters below (Earth) (Genesis 1:6–8). We have told here the story of the Tower of Babel. Man must not try to become God. A person must learn to trust God to take care of him. The people in the story are afraid God will separate them and thus try to make a name for themselves and become gods themselves. This does not mean that a person must not strive for more, but that he must not always be dissatisfied and afraid. People often want to build taller and taller buildings, climb higher and higher mountains. They worship idols rather than God. The question is, why? Sometimes in striving for more, one ends up with less and brings about what he is trying to destroy. People in this story cannot accept that God is taking care of them but really want to replace God. They do not accept the separation between Heaven and Earth.

On the third day of creation, God separates dry land (Earth) from waters (Seas) and creates vegetation (Genesis 1:9–13). Here we have told the story of Noah and the flood. God is described as so upset with the immoral behavior of the people He has created that He breaks down the division between dry land and waters. Many cultures have a flood story, probably reflecting the end of an ice age in which many lands may have been overrun by oceans. We may be experiencing a similar phenomenon today with fears of global warming. Note, however, the particular point that the biblical story makes of this phenomenon. It is God's response to the immorality of man that leads to the flood. Yet, at the same time, God provides the blueprint for an ark for Noah, who was described as a righteous man. And God instructs Noah to bring male and female of each species on the ark, allowing each species, including human beings, to replenish the world through union of male and female. Note also that God puts a rainbow in the sky as a sign that there will be no more floods. These are important lessons for a child.

On the fourth day of creation, God creates two lights in the sky: the sun for day and the moon for night (Genesis 1:14–19). Here we tell the story of Abraham leaving his father's house after rejecting the worship of idols. Abraham realizes that neither the sun nor the moon should be worshiped per se, but that both are created by God. This is important for a child to understand. Many things that glitter brightly seem to be all-encompassing but are really less important than the force that has created them. Stars, the sun, and the moon can certainly be enjoyed but are not to be worshiped. With all sorts of quick solutions and elaborate promises in our culture, this is a really important point for a child to learn.

On the fifth day of creation, God creates the birds, sea creatures, and insects (living creatures that creep) (Genesis 1:20–23). Here we tell the story of Jonah and the big fish to illustrate how God's creature, a fish, saves the life of Jonah. Jonah is asked to go on a mission to the people of Nineveh to warn them to change their ways. Jonah does not want to go because he does not think the people should be saved. On the other hand, he does not want to disobey God either. So he runs away to Tarshish by ship. God sends a storm and the ship is endangered. Jonah tells his shipmates that he is the cause of the storm and to throw him overboard. But God sends a big fish to swallow him and save him from drowning and give him time to slowly mature. This story illustrates how God's creatures can be very important in His plan for mankind and that the human being is in a very special relationship with animals of all kind. This theme is further developed in our next story illustrating, the sixth day of creation.

On the sixth day of creation, God creates the animals and finally human beings in the likeness of God, and gives human beings dominion over all living creatures (Genesis 1:24–28). We illustrate this day with the story of God giving Adam the job of naming the animals. This is a very important lesson for a child. Naming something personalizes it and implies a responsibility to care for it. So if a child has a pet, he gives it a name and then is in a very special relationship with it. He feeds it, keeps it clean, watches that it has shelter and does not run away. He takes it for walks, pets it, plays with it, and generally does all he can to make the pet content and happy. This is important training for a child when he himself becomes a parent and takes care of his own children. Additionally, children can examine ways that they care for others—other people, animals, and even the environment.

Finally, on the seventh day of creation, God rests, and human beings must also (Genesis 2:1–4). The importance of rest is a very important lesson for children to learn, as they often play so hard that they become overtired and crabby. We illustrate this principle with the story of Elijah. Elijah strives very strongly for God against forces that seem to him to be completely immoral. Elijah tries very hard to prove God is the one by using force and might. He eventually exhausts himself and falls into despair. He then rests and is given food and drink. He learns that in rest and stillness he is able to rejuvenate himself. In rest and stillness, truth, and strength come through most clearly. Elijah to continues represent this message to us by returning to us at times of eating and rejuvenation such as the Passover Seder, and at times of recognizing quiet good deeds such as his appearing incognito as an old man. Finally, he is said to come back during messianic time, as a symbol of peace. The importance of rest as a key to self-understanding and the rejuvenation that comes with it is a very important lesson for a child to learn. It is important to be active in life. But, likewise, it is important to rest at times also.

All these stories are designed to help enhance a child's Emotional Quotient (EQ). Maturity cannot be measured simply by intellectual ability alone but depends also on life wisdom. There is no better place to look for this wisdom than the Hebrew Bible itself, the Book of Books.

Appendix

Biblical Spark for Day One: David and Goliath
1 Samuel Chapter 17

1 Now the Philistines gathered together their armies to battle, and they were gathered together at Socoh, which belongeth to Judah, and pitched between Socoh and Azekah, in Ephes-dammim. **2** And Saul and the men of Israel were gathered together, and pitched in the vale of Elah, and set the battle in array against the Philistines. **3** And the Philistines stood on the mountain on the one side, and Israel stood on the mountain on the other side; and there was a valley between them. **4** And there went out a champion from the camp of the Philistines, named Goliath, of Gath, whose height was six cubits and a span. **5** And he had a helmet of brass upon his head, and he was clad with a coat of mail; and the weight of the coat was five thousand shekels of brass. **6** And he had greaves of brass upon his legs, and a javelin of brass between his shoulders. **7** And the shaft of his spear was like a weaver's beam; and his spear's head weighed six hundred shekels of iron; and his shield-bearer went before him. **8** Goliath stood and cried unto the armies of Israel, and said unto them: 'Why do ye come out to set your battle in array? am not I a Philistine, and ye servants to Saul? choose you a man for you, and let him come down to me. **9** If he be able to fight with me, and kill me, then will we be your servants; but if I prevail against him, and kill him, then shall ye be our servants, and serve us.' **10** And the Philistine said: 'I do taunt the armies of Israel this day; give me a man, that we may fight together.' **11** And when Saul and all Israel heard those words of the Philistine, they were dismayed, and greatly afraid.

12 Now David was the son of that Ephrathite of Beth-lehem in Judah, whose name was Jesse; and he had eight sons; and the man was an old man in the days of Saul, stricken in years among men. **13** And the three eldest sons of Jesse had gone after Saul to the battle; and the names of his three sons that went to the battle were Eliab the first-born, and next unto him Abinadab, and the third Shammah. **14** And David was the youngest; and the three eldest followed Saul. **15** Now David went to and fro from Saul to feed his father's sheep at Beth-lehem. **16** And the Philistine drew near morning and evening, and presented himself forty days.

17 And Jesse said unto David his son: 'Take now for thy brethren an ephah of this parched corn, and these ten loaves, and carry them quickly to the camp to thy brethren. **18** And bring these ten cheeses unto the captain of their thousand, and to thy brethren shalt thou bring greetings, and take their pledge; **19** now Saul, and they, and all the men of Israel, are in the vale of Elah, fighting with the Philistines.' **20** And David rose up early in the morning, and left the sheep with a keeper, and took, and went, as Jesse had commanded him; and he came to the barricade, as the host which was going forth to the fight shouted for the battle. **21** And Israel and the Philistines put the battle in array, army against army. **22** And David left his baggage in the hand of the keeper of the baggage, and ran to the army, and came and greeted his brethren. **23** And as he talked with them, behold, there came up the champion, the Philistine of Gath, Goliath by name, out of the ranks of the Philistines, and spoke according to the same words; and David heard them. **24** And all the men of Israel, when they saw the man, fled from him, and were sore afraid. **25** And the men of Israel said: 'Have ye seen this man that is come up? surely to taunt Israel is he come up; and it shall be, that the man who killeth him, the king will enrich him with great riches, and will give him his daughter, and make his father's house free in Israel.'

26 And David spoke to the men that stood by him, saying: 'What shall be done to the man that killeth this Philistine, and taketh away the taunt from Israel? for who is this uncircumcised Philistine, that he should have taunted the armies of the living God?' **27** And the people answered him after this manner, saying: 'So shall it be done to the man that killeth him.' **28** And Eliab his eldest brother heard when he spoke unto the men; and Eliab's anger was kindled against David, and he said: 'Why art thou come down? and with whom hast thou left those few sheep in the wilderness? I know thy presumptuousness, and the naughtiness of thy heart; for thou art come down that thou mightest see the battle.' **29** And David said: 'What have I now done? Was it not but a word?' **30** And he turned away from him toward another, and spoke after the same manner; and the people answered him after the former manner. **31** And when the words were heard which David spoke, they rehearsed them before Saul; and he was taken to him.

32 And David said to Saul: 'Let no man's heart fail within him; thy servant will go and fight with this Philistine.' **33** And Saul said to David: 'Thou art not able to go against this Philistine to fight with him; for thou art but a youth, and he a man of war from his youth.' **34** And David said unto Saul: 'Thy servant kept his father's sheep; and when there came a lion, or a bear, and took a lamb out of the flock, **35** I went out after him, and smote him, and delivered it out of his mouth; and when he arose against me, I caught him by his beard, and smote him, and slew him. **36** Thy servant smote both the lion and the bear; and this uncircumcised Philistine shall be as one of them, seeing he hath taunted the armies of the living God.' **37** And David said: 'The LORD that delivered me out of the paw of the lion, and out of the paw of the bear, He will deliver me out of the hand of this Philistine.' And Saul said unto David: 'Go, and the LORD shall be with thee.'

38 And Saul clad David with his apparel, and he put a helmet of brass upon his head, and he clad him with a coat of mail. **39** And David girded his sword upon his apparel, and he essayed to go, [but could not]; for he had not tried it. And David said unto Saul: 'I cannot go with these; for I have not tried them.' And David put them off him. **40** And he took his staff in his hand, and chose him five smooth stones out of the brook, and put them in the shepherd's bag which he had, even in his scrip; and his sling was in his hand; and he drew near to the Philistine. **41** And the Philistine came nearer and nearer unto David; and the man that bore the shield went before him. **42** And when the Philistine looked about, and saw David, he disdained him; for he was but a youth, and ruddy, and withal of a fair countenance. **43** And the Philistine said unto David: 'Am I a dog, that thou comest to me with staves?' And the Philistine cursed David by his god. **44** And the Philistine said to David: 'Come to me, and I will give thy flesh unto the fowls of the air, and to the beasts of the field.'

45 Then said David to the Philistine: 'Thou comest to me with a sword, and with a spear, and with a javelin; but I come to thee in the name of the LORD of hosts, the God of the armies of Israel, whom thou hast taunted. **46** This day will the LORD deliver thee into my hand; and I will smite thee, and take thy head from off thee; and I will give the carcasses of the host of the Philistines this day unto the fowls of the air, and to the wild beasts of the earth; that all the earth may know that there is a God in Israel; **47** and that all this assembly may know that the LORD saveth not with sword and spear; for the battle is the LORD'S, and He will give you into our hand.' **48** And it came to pass, when the Philistine arose, and came and drew nigh to meet David, that David hastened, and ran toward the army to meet the Philistine. **49** And David put his hand in his bag, and took thence a stone, and slung it, and smote the Philistine in his forehead; and the stone sank into his forehead, and he fell upon his face to the earth. **50** So David prevailed over the Philistine with a sling and with a stone, and smote the Philistine, and slew him; but there was no sword in the hand of David. **51** And David ran, and stood over the Philistine, and took his sword, and drew it out of the sheath thereof, and slew him, and cut off his head therewith. And when the Philistines saw that their mighty man was dead, they fled.

52 And the men of Israel and of Judah arose, and shouted, and pursued the Philistines, until thou comest to Gai, and to the gates of Ekron. And the wounded of the Philistines fell down by the way to Shaaraim, even unto Gath, and unto Ekron. **53** And the children of Israel returned from chasing after the Philistines, and they spoiled their camp. 54 And David took the head of the Philistine, and brought it to Jerusalem; but he put his armour in his tent. **55** And when Saul saw David go forth against the Philistine, he said unto Abner, the captain of the host: 'Abner, whose son is this youth?' And Abner said: 'As thy soul liveth, O king, I cannot tell.' **56** And the king said: 'Inquire thou whose son the stripling is.'

57 And as David returned from the slaughter of the Philistine, Abner took him, and brought him before Saul with the head of the Philistine in his hand. **58** And Saul said to him: 'Whose son art thou, thou young man?' And David answered: 'I am the son of thy servant Jesse the Beth-lehemite.'

Biblical Spark for Day Two: The Tower of Babel
Genesis Chapter 11

1 And the whole earth was of one language and of one speech. **2** And it came to pass, as they journeyed east, that they found a plain in the land of Shinar; and they dwelt there. **3** And they said one to another: 'Come, let us make brick, and burn them thoroughly.' And they had brick for stone, and slime had they for mortar. **4** And they said: 'Come, let us build us a city, and a tower, with its top in heaven, and let us make us a name; lest we be scattered abroad upon the face of the whole earth.'

5 And the LORD came down to see the city and the tower, which the children of men builded. **6** And the LORD said: 'Behold, they are one people, and they have all one language; and this is what they begin to do; and now nothing will be withholden from them, which they purpose to do. **7** Come, let us go down, and there confound their language, that they may not understand one another's speech.'

8 So the LORD scattered them abroad from thence upon the face of all the earth; and they left off to build the city. **9** Therefore was the name of it called Babel; because the LORD did there confound the language of all the earth; and from thence did the LORD scatter them abroad upon the face of all the earth.

Biblical Spark for Day Three: Noah and the Flood
Genesis Chapters 6–9

Genesis Chapter 6

5 And the LORD saw that the wickedness of man was great in the earth, and that every imagination of the thoughts of his heart was only evil continually. **6** And it repented the LORD that He had made man on the earth, and it grieved Him at His heart. **7** And the LORD said: 'I will blot out man whom I have created from the face of the earth; both man, and beast, and creeping thing, and fowl of the air; for it repenteth Me that I have made them.' **8** But Noah found grace in the eyes of the LORD.

9 These are the generations of Noah. Noah was in his generations a man righteous and whole-hearted; Noah walked with God. **10** And Noah begot three sons, Shem, Ham, and Japheth. **11** And the earth was corrupt before God, and the earth was filled with violence. **12** And God saw the earth, and, behold, it was corrupt; for all flesh had corrupted their way upon the earth. **13** And God said unto Noah: 'The end of all flesh is come before Me; for the earth is filled with violence through them; and, behold, I will destroy them with the earth. **14** Make thee an ark of gopher wood; with rooms shalt thou make the ark, and shalt pitch it within and without with pitch. **15** And this is how thou shalt make it: the length of the ark three hundred cubits, the breadth of it fifty cubits, and the height of it thirty cubits. **16** A light shalt thou make to the ark, and to a cubit shalt thou finish it upward; and the door of the ark shalt thou set in the side thereof; with lower, second, and third stories shalt thou make it. **17** And I, behold, I do bring the flood of waters upon the earth, to destroy all flesh, wherein is the breath of life, from under heaven; every thing that is in the earth shall perish.

18 But I will establish My covenant with thee; and thou shalt come into the ark, thou, and thy sons, and thy wife, and thy sons' wives with thee. **19** And of every living thing of all flesh, two of every sort shalt thou bring into the ark, to keep them alive with thee; they shall be male and female. **20** Of the fowl after their kind, and of the cattle after their kind, of every creeping thing of the ground after its kind, two of every sort shall come unto thee, to keep them alive. **21** And take thou unto thee of all food that is eaten, and gather it to thee; and it shall be for food for thee, and for them.' **22** Thus did Noah; according to all that God commanded him, so did he.

Genesis Chapter 7

1 And the LORD said unto Noah: 'Come thou and all thy house into the ark; for thee have I seen righteous before Me in this generation. **2** Of every clean beast thou shalt take to thee seven and seven, each with his mate; and of the beasts that are not clean two [and two], each with his mate; **3** of the fowl also of the air, seven and seven, male and female; to keep seed alive upon the face of all the earth. **4** For yet seven days, and I will cause it to rain upon the earth forty days and forty nights; and every living substance that I have made will I blot out from off the face of the earth.'

5 And Noah did according unto all that the LORD commanded him. **6** And Noah was six hundred years old when the flood of waters was upon the earth. **7** And Noah went in, and his sons, and his wife, and his sons' wives with him, into the ark, because of the waters of the flood. **8** Of clean beasts, and of beasts that are not clean, and of fowls, and of every thing that creepeth upon the ground, **9** there went in two and two unto Noah into the ark, male and female, as God commanded Noah. **10** And it came to pass after the seven days, that the waters of the flood were upon the earth. **11** In the six hundredth year of Noah's life, in the second month, on the seventeenth day of the month, on the same day were all the fountains of the great deep broken up, and the windows of heaven were opened. **12** And the rain was upon the earth forty days and forty nights. **13** In the selfsame day entered Noah, and Shem, and Ham, and Japheth, the sons of Noah, and Noah's wife, and the three wives of his sons with them, into the ark; **14** they, and every beast after its kind, and all the cattle after their kind, and every creeping thing that creepeth upon the earth after its kind, and every fowl after its kind, every bird of every sort. **15** And they went in unto Noah into the ark, two and two of all flesh wherein is the breath of life. **16** And they that went in, went in male and female of all flesh, as God commanded him; and the LORD shut him in.

17 And the flood was forty days upon the earth; and the waters increased, and bore up the ark, and it was lifted up above the earth. **18** And the waters prevailed, and increased greatly upon the earth; and the ark went upon the face of the waters. **19** And the waters prevailed exceedingly upon the earth; and all the high mountains that were under the whole heaven were covered. **20** Fifteen cubits upward did the waters prevail; and the mountains were covered. **21** And all flesh perished that moved upon the earth, both fowl, and cattle, and beast, and every swarming thing that swarmeth upon the earth, and every man; **22** all in whose nostrils was the breath of the spirit of life, whatsoever was in the dry land, died. **23** And He blotted out every living substance which was upon the face of the ground, both man, and cattle, and creeping thing, and fowl of the heaven; and they were blotted out from the earth; and Noah only was left, and they that were with him in the ark. **24** And the waters prevailed upon the earth a hundred and fifty days.

Genesis Chapter 8

1 And God remembered Noah, and every living thing, and all the cattle that were with him in the ark; and God made a wind to pass over the earth, and the waters assuaged; **2** the fountains also of the deep and the windows of heaven were stopped, and the rain from heaven was restrained. **3** And the waters returned from off the earth continually; and after the end of a hundred and fifty days the waters decreased. **4** And the ark rested in the seventh month, on the seventeenth day of the month, upon the mountains of Ararat. **5** And the waters decreased continually until the tenth month; in the tenth month, on the first day of the month, were the tops of the mountains seen.

6 And it came to pass at the end of forty days, that Noah opened the window of the ark which he had made. **7** And he sent forth a raven, and it went forth to and fro, until the waters were dried up from off the earth. **8** And he sent forth a dove from him, to see if the waters were abated from off the face of the ground. **9** But the dove found no rest for the sole of her foot, and she returned unto him to the ark, for the waters were on the face of the whole earth; and he put forth his hand, and took her, and brought her in unto him into the ark. **10** And he stayed yet other seven days; and again he sent forth the dove out of the ark. **11** And the dove came in to him at eventide; and lo in her mouth an olive-leaf freshly plucked; so Noah knew that the waters were abated from off the earth. **12** And he stayed yet other seven days; and sent forth the dove; and she returned not again unto him any more.

13 And it came to pass in the six hundred and first year, in the first month, the first day of the month, the waters were dried up from off the earth; and Noah removed the covering of the ark, and looked, and behold, the face of the ground was dried. **14** And in the second month, on the seven and twentieth day of the month, was the earth dry. **15** And God spoke unto Noah, saying: **16** 'Go forth from the ark, thou, and thy wife, and thy sons, and thy sons' wives with thee. **17** Bring forth with thee every living thing that is with thee of all flesh, both fowl, and cattle, and every creeping thing that creepeth upon the earth; that they may swarm in the earth, and be fruitful, and multiply upon the earth.' **18** And Noah went forth, and his sons, and his wife, and his sons' wives with him; **19** every beast, every creeping thing, and every fowl, whatsoever moveth upon the earth, after their families; went forth out of the ark.

20 And Noah builded an altar unto the LORD; and took of every clean beast, and of every clean fowl, and offered burnt-offerings on the altar. **21** And the LORD smelled the sweet savour; and the LORD said in His heart: 'I will not again curse the ground any more for man's sake; for the imagination of man's heart is evil from his youth; neither will I again smite any more every thing living, as I have done. **22** While the earth remaineth, seedtime and harvest, and cold and heat, and summer and winter, and day and night shall not cease.'

Genesis Chapter 9

1 And God blessed Noah and his sons, and said unto them: 'Be fruitful and multiply, and replenish the earth. **2** And the fear of you and the dread of you shall be upon every beast of the earth, and upon every fowl of the air, and upon all wherewith the ground teemeth, and upon all the fishes of the sea: into your hand are they delivered. **3** Every moving thing that liveth shall be for food for you; as the green herb have I given you all. **4** Only flesh with the life thereof, which is the blood thereof, shall ye not eat. **5** And surely your blood of your lives will I require; at the hand of every beast will I require it; and at the hand of man, even at the hand of every man's brother, will I require the life of man. **6** Whoso sheddeth man's blood, by man shall his blood be shed; for in the image of God made He man. **7** And you, be ye fruitful, and multiply; swarm in the earth, and multiply therein.'

8 And God spoke unto Noah, and to his sons with him, saying: **9** 'As for Me, behold, I establish My covenant with you, and with your seed after you; **10** and with every living creature that is with you, the fowl, the cattle, and every beast of the earth with you; of all that go out of the ark, even every beast of the earth. **11** And I will establish My covenant with you; neither shall all flesh be cut off any more by the waters of the flood; neither shall there any more be a flood to destroy the earth.' **12** And God said: 'This is the token of the covenant which I make between Me and you and every living creature that is with you, for perpetual generations: **13** I have set My bow in the cloud, and it shall be for a token of a covenant between Me and the earth. **14** And it shall come to pass, when I bring clouds over the earth, and the bow is seen in the cloud, **15** that I will remember My covenant, which is between Me and you and every living creature of all flesh; and the waters shall no more become a flood to destroy all flesh. **16** And the bow shall be in the cloud; and I will look upon it, that I may remember the everlasting covenant between God and every living creature of all flesh that is upon the earth.' **17** And God said unto Noah: 'This is the token of the covenant which I have established between Me and all flesh that is upon the earth.'

Biblical Spark for Day Four: Abraham Against Idolatry
Sefer ha-Aggadah 3

Sefer ha-Aggadah 3:4

…When Abraham was three years old, he went out of the cave and observing the world wondered in his heart: Who created heaven and earth and me? All that day he prayed to the sun. In the evening, the sun set in the west and the moon rose in the east. Upon seeing the moon and the stars around it, he said: This one must have created heaven and earth and me—these stars must be the moon's princes and courtiers. So all night long he stood in prayer to the moon. In the morning, the moon sank in the west and the sun rose in the east. Then he said: "There is no might in either of these. There must be a higher Lord over them—to Him will I pray, and before Him will I prostrate myself." (Bet ha Midrash 2: 118–196)

Sefer ha-Aggadah 3:8

Abraham's family used to make images and sell them in the market. One day, when it was Abraham's turn to sell, his father Terah gave him several baskets of household gods and set him up in the marketplace. A man came to him and asked: "Have you a god to sell?" Abraham: "What kind of god do you wish to buy?" The man: "I am a mighty man—give me a god as mighty as I am." So Abraham took an image that was standing on a shelf higher than all the others and said: "Pay the money and take this one." The man asked: "Is this god as mighty as I am?" Abraham replied: "You good-for-nothing! Don't you know the way of gods? The one who sits above all others is the mightiest of all…"

Then Abraham took all the gods and brought them back to his father Terah. Terah's other sons said to their father: "This Abraham does not know how to sell gods; come, then, and let us make him a priest." Abraham asked: "What is a priest's work?" They replied: "He waits upon the gods, offers sacrifice to them, and serves them food and drink." So they made him priest. Abraham promptly set food and drink before the images and said to them: "Come and eat, come and drink so that you may be able to bestow good on human beings." But not one of them took anything at all to eat or drink. Then Abraham began to recite the verse "They have mouths but they speak not; eyes have they, but they see not; they have ears, but they hear not; noses have they, but they smell not; they have hands, but they handle not; feet have they, but they walk not." (Psalms 115: 5–7)

A woman came carrying a bowl of fine flour and said: "Here, offer it to the gods." At that, Abraham seized a stick, smashed all the images, and placed the stick in the hand of the biggest of them. When his father came, he asked: "Who did this to the gods?" Abraham answered: "Would I hide anything from my father? A woman came with a bowl of fine flour and said: Here, offer it up to them. When I offered it, one god said, 'I will eat first,' and another said, 'No, I will eat first.' Then the biggest of them rose up and smashed all the others." His father replied: "Are you making sport of me? They cannot do anything!" Abraham answered: "You say you cannot. Let your ears hear what your mouth is saying."

Biblical Spark for Day Five: Jonah and the Great Fish
Jonah

Jonah Chapter 1

1 Now the word of the LORD came unto Jonah the son of Amittai, saying: **2** 'Arise, go to Nineveh, that great city, and proclaim against it; for their wickedness is come up before Me.' **3** But Jonah rose up to flee unto Tarshish from the presence of the LORD; and he went down to Joppa, and found a ship going to Tarshish; so he paid the fare thereof, and went down into it, to go with them unto Tarshish, from the presence of the LORD.

4 But the LORD hurled a great wind into the sea, and there was a mighty tempest in the sea, so that the ship was like to be broken. **5** And the mariners were afraid, and cried every man unto his god; and they cast forth the wares that were in the ship into the sea, to lighten it unto them. But Jonah was gone down into the innermost parts of the ship; and he lay, and was fast asleep. **6** So the shipmaster came to him, and said unto him: 'What meanest thou that thou sleepest? arise, call upon thy God, if so be that God will think upon us, that we perish not.'

7 And they said every one to his fellow: 'Come, and let us cast lots, that we may know for whose cause this evil is upon us.' So they cast lots, and the lot fell upon Jonah. 8 Then said they unto him: 'Tell us, we pray thee, for whose cause this evil is upon us: what is thine occupation? and whence comest thou? what is thy country? and of what people art thou?' 9 And he said unto them: 'I am an Hebrew; and I fear the LORD, the God of heaven, who hath made the sea and the dry land.' 10 Then were the men exceedingly afraid, and said unto him: 'What is this that thou hast done?' For the men knew that he fled from the presence of the LORD, because he had told them.

11 Then said they unto him: 'What shall we do unto thee, that the sea may be calm unto us?' for the sea grew more and more tempestuous. 12 And he said unto them: 'Take me up, and cast me forth into the sea; so shall the sea be calm unto you; for I know that for my sake this great tempest is upon you.' 13 Nevertheless the men rowed hard to bring it to the land; but they could not; for the sea grew more and more tempestuous against them. 14 Wherefore they cried unto the LORD, and said: 'We beseech Thee, O LORD, we beseech Thee, let us not perish for this man's life, and lay not upon us innocent blood; for Thou, O LORD, hast done as it pleased Thee.' 15 So they took up Jonah, and cast him forth into the sea; and the sea ceased from its raging. 16 Then the men feared the LORD exceedingly; and they offered a sacrifice unto the LORD, and made vows.

Jonah Chapter 2

1 And the LORD prepared a great fish to swallow up Jonah; and Jonah was in the belly of the fish three days and three nights. 2 Then Jonah prayed unto the LORD his God out of the fish's belly. 3 And he said: I called out of mine affliction unto the LORD, and He answered me; out of the belly of the nether-world cried I, and Thou heardest my voice. 4 For Thou didst cast me into the depth, in the heart of the seas, and the flood was round about me; all Thy waves and Thy billows passed over me. 5 And I said: 'I am cast out from before Thine eyes; yet I will look again toward Thy holy temple. 6 The waters compassed me about, even to the soul; the deep was round about me; the weeds were wrapped about my head. 7 I went down to the bottoms of the mountains; the earth with her bars closed upon me for ever; yet hast Thou brought up my life from the pit, O LORD my God. 8 When my soul fainted within me, I remembered the LORD; and my prayer came in unto Thee, into Thy holy temple. 9 They that regard lying vanities forsake their own mercy. 10 But I will sacrifice unto Thee with the voice of thanksgiving; that which I have vowed I will pay. Salvation is of the LORD.' 11 And the LORD spoke unto the fish, and it vomited out Jonah upon the dry land.

Jonah Chapter 3

1 And the word of the LORD came unto Jonah the second time, saying: **2** 'Arise, go unto Nineveh, that great city, and make unto it the proclamation that I bid thee.' **3** So Jonah arose, and went unto Nineveh, according to the word of the LORD. Now Nineveh was an exceeding great city, of three days' journey. **4** And Jonah began to enter into the city a day's journey, and he proclaimed, and said: 'Yet forty days, and Nineveh shall be overthrown.' **5** And the people of Nineveh believed God; and they proclaimed a fast, and put on sackcloth, from the greatest of them even to the least of them.

6 And the tidings reached the king of Nineveh, and he arose from his throne, and laid his robe from him, and covered him with sackcloth, and sat in ashes. **7** And he caused it to be proclaimed and published through Nineveh by the decree of the king and his nobles, saying: 'Let neither man nor beast, herd nor flock, taste any thing; let them not feed, nor drink water; **8** but let them be covered with sackcloth, both man and beast, and let them cry mightily unto God; yea, let them turn every one from his evil way, and from the violence that is in their hands. **9** Who knoweth whether God will not turn and repent, and turn away from His fierce anger, that we perish not?' **10** And God saw their works, that they turned from their evil way; and God repented of the evil, which He said He would do unto them; and He did it not.

Jonah Chapter 4

1 But it displeased Jonah exceedingly, and he was angry. **2** And he prayed unto the LORD, and said: 'I pray Thee, O LORD, was not this my saying, when I was yet in mine own country? Therefore I fled beforehand unto Tarshish; for I knew that Thou art a gracious God, and compassionate, long-suffering, and abundant in mercy, and repentest Thee of the evil. **3** Therefore now, O LORD, take, I beseech Thee, my life from me; for it is better for me to die than to live.' **4** And the LORD said: 'Art thou greatly angry?'

5 Then Jonah went out of the city, and sat on the east side of the city, and there made him a booth, and sat under it in the shadow, till he might see what would become of the city. **6** And the LORD God prepared a gourd, and made it to come up over Jonah, that it might be a shadow over his head, to deliver him from his evil. So Jonah was exceeding glad because of the gourd. **7** But God prepared a worm when the morning rose the next day, and it smote the gourd, that it withered. **8** And it came to pass, when the sun arose, that God prepared a vehement east wind; and the sun beat upon the head of Jonah, that he fainted, and requested for himself that he might die, and said: 'It is better for me to die than to live.' **9** And God said to Jonah: 'Art thou greatly angry for the gourd?' And he said: 'I am greatly angry, even unto death.' **10** And the LORD said: 'Thou hast had pity on the gourd, for which thou hast not laboured, neither madest it grow, which came up in a night, and perished in a night; **11** and should not I have pity on Nineveh, that great city, wherein are more than sixscore thousand persons that cannot discern between their right hand and their left hand, and also much cattle?'

Biblical Spark for Day Six: Adam Names the Animals
Genesis Chapter 2

Genesis Chapter 1

26 And God said, Let us make man in our image, after our likeness: and let them have dominion over the fish of the sea, and over the fowl of the air, and over the cattle, and over all the earth, and over every creeping thing that creepeth upon the earth. **27** So God created man in his own image, in the image of God created he him; male and female created he them. **28** And God blessed them, and God said unto them, Be fruitful, and multiply, and replenish the earth, and subdue it: and have dominion over the fish of the sea, and over the fowl of the air, and over every living thing that moveth upon the earth. **29** And God said, Behold, I have given you every herb bearing seed, which is upon the face of all the earth, and every tree, in the which is the fruit of a tree yielding seed; to you it shall be for meat. **30** And to every beast of the earth, and to every fowl of the air, and to every thing that creepeth upon the earth, wherein there is life, I have given every green herb for meat: and it was so.

Genesis Chapter 2

18 And the LORD God said: 'It is not good that the man should be alone; I will make him a helpmeet for him.' **19** And out of the ground the LORD God formed every beast of the field, and every fowl of the air; and brought them unto the man to see what he would call them; and whatsoever the man would call every living creature, that was to be the name thereof. **20** And the man gave names to all cattle, and to the fowl of the air, and to every beast of the field; but for Adam there was not found a helpmeet for him.

Biblical Spark for Day Seven: The Sabbath: Elijah Rests
1 Kings Chapters 17–19

1 Kings Chapter 17

1 And Elijah the Tishbite, who was of the settlers of Gilead, said unto Ahab: 'As the LORD, the God of Israel, liveth, before whom I stand, there shall not be dew nor rain these years, but according to my word.' **2** And the word of the LORD came unto him, saying: **3** 'Get thee hence, and turn thee eastward, and hide thyself by the brook Cherith, that is before the Jordan. **4** And it shall be, that thou shalt drink of the brook; and I have commanded the ravens to feed thee there.' **5** So he went and did according unto the word of the LORD; for he went and dwelt by the brook Cherith, that is before the Jordan.

6 And the ravens brought him bread and flesh in the morning, and bread and flesh in the evening; and he drank of the brook. **7** And it came to pass after a while, that the brook dried up, because there was no rain in the land.

8 And the word of the LORD came unto him, saying: **9** 'Arise, get thee to Zarephath, which belongeth to Zidon, and dwell there; behold, I have commanded a widow there to sustain thee.' **10** So he arose and went to Zarephath; and when he came to the gate of the city, behold, a widow was there gathering sticks; and he called to her, and said: 'Fetch me, I pray thee, a little water in a vessel, that I may drink.' **11** And as she was going to fetch it, he called to her, and said: 'Bring me, I pray thee, a morsel of bread in thy hand.' **12** And she said: 'As the LORD thy God liveth, I have not a cake, only a handful of meal in the jar, and a little oil in the cruse; and, behold, I am gathering two sticks, that I may go in and dress it for me and my son, that we may eat it, and die.' **13** And Elijah said unto her: 'Fear not; go and do as thou hast said; but make me thereof a little cake first, and bring it forth unto me, and afterward make for thee and for thy son. **14** For thus saith the LORD, the God of Israel: The jar of meal shall not be spent, neither shall the cruse of oil fail, until the day that the LORD sendeth rain upon the land.' **15** And she went and did according to the saying of Elijah; and she, and he, and her house, did eat many days. **16** The jar of meal was not spent, neither did the cruse of oil fail, according to the word of the LORD, which He spoke by Elijah.

17 And it came to pass after these things, that the son of the woman, the mistress of the house, fell sick; and his sickness was so sore, that there was no breath left in him. **18** And she said unto Elijah: 'What have I to do with thee, O thou man of God? art thou come unto me to bring my sin to remembrance, and to slay my son?' **19** And he said unto her: 'Give me thy son.' And he took him out of her bosom, and carried him up into the upper chamber, where he abode, and laid him upon his own bed. **20** And he cried unto the LORD, and said: 'O LORD my God, hast Thou also brought evil upon the widow with whom I sojourn, by slaying her son?' **21** And he stretched himself upon the child three times, and cried unto the LORD, and said: 'O LORD my God, I pray thee, let this child's soul come back into him.' **22** And the LORD hearkened unto the voice of Elijah; and the soul of the child came back into him, and he revived. **23** And Elijah took the child, and brought him down out of the upper chamber into the house, and delivered him unto his mother; and Elijah said: 'See, thy son liveth.' **24** And the woman said to Elijah: 'Now I know that thou art a man of God, and that the word of the LORD in thy mouth is truth.'

1 Kings Chapter 18

1 And it came to pass after many days, that the word of the LORD came to Elijah, in the third year, saying: 'Go, show thyself unto Ahab, and I will send rain upon the land.' **2** And Elijah went to show himself unto Ahab. And the famine was sore in Samaria. **3** And Ahab called Obadiah, who was over the household.—Now Obadiah feared the LORD greatly; **4** for it was so, when Jezebel cut off the prophets of the LORD, that Obadiah took a hundred prophets, and hid them fifty in a cave, and fed them with bread and water. **5** And Ahab said unto Obadiah: 'Go through the land, unto all the springs of water, and unto all the brooks; peradventure we may find grass and save the horses and mules alive, that we lose not all the beasts.' **6** So they divided the land between them to pass throughout it: Ahab went one way by himself, and Obadiah went another way by himself.

7 And as Obadiah was in the way, behold, Elijah met him; and he knew him, and fell on his face, and said: 'Is it thou, my lord Elijah?' **8** And he answered him: 'It is I; go, tell thy lord: Behold, Elijah is here.' **9** And he said: 'Wherein have I sinned, that thou wouldest deliver thy servant into the hand of Ahab, to slay me? **10** As the LORD thy God liveth, there is no nation or kingdom, whither my lord hath not sent to seek thee; and when they said: He is not here, he took an oath of the kingdom and nation, that they found thee not. **11** And now thou sayest: Go, tell thy lord: Behold, Elijah is here. **12** And it will come to pass, as soon as I am gone from thee, that the spirit of the LORD will carry thee whither I know not; and so when I come and tell Ahab, and he cannot find thee, he will slay me; but I thy servant fear the LORD from my youth. **13** Was it not told my lord what I did when Jezebel slew the prophets of the LORD, how I hid a hundred men of the LORD'S prophets by fifty in a cave, and fed them with bread and water? **14** And now thou sayest: Go, tell thy lord: Behold, Elijah is here; and he will slay me.' **15** And Elijah said: 'As the LORD of hosts liveth, before whom I stand, I will surely show myself unto him to-day.'

16 So Obadiah went to meet Ahab, and told him; and Ahab went to meet Elijah. **17** And it came to pass, when Ahab saw Elijah, that Ahab said unto him: 'Is it thou, thou troubler of Israel?' **18** And he answered: 'I have not troubled Israel; but thou, and thy father's house, in that ye have forsaken the commandments of the LORD, and thou hast followed the Baalim. **19** Now therefore send, and gather to me all Israel unto mount Carmel, and the prophets of Baal four hundred and fifty, and the prophets of the Asherah four hundred, that eat at Jezebel's table.' **20** And Ahab sent unto all the children of Israel, and gathered the prophets together unto mount Carmel. **21** And Elijah came near unto all the people, and said: 'How long halt ye between two opinions? if the LORD be God, follow Him; but if Baal, follow him.' And the people answered him not a word.

22 Then said Elijah unto the people: 'I, even I only, am left a prophet of the LORD; but Baal's prophets are four hundred and fifty men. **23** Let them therefore give us two bullocks; and let them choose one bullock for themselves, and cut it in pieces, and lay it on the wood, and put no fire under; and I will dress the other bullock, and lay it on the wood, and put no fire under. **24** And call ye on the name of your god, and I will call on the name of the LORD; and the God that answereth by fire, let him be God.' And all the people answered and said: 'It is well spoken.'

25 And Elijah said unto the prophets of Baal: 'Choose you one bullock for yourselves, and dress it first; for ye are many; and call on the name of your god, but put no fire under.' **26** And they took the bullock which was given them, and they dressed it, and called on the name of Baal from morning even until noon, saying: 'O Baal, answer us.' But there was no voice, nor any that answered. And they danced in halting wise about the altar which was made. **27** And it came to pass at noon, that Elijah mocked them, and said: 'Cry aloud; for he is a god; either he is musing, or he is gone aside, or he is in a journey, or peradventure he sleepeth, and must be awaked.' **28** And they cried aloud, and cut themselves after their manner with swords and lances, till the blood gushed out upon them. **29** And it was so, when midday was past, that they prophesied until the time of the offering of the evening offering; but their was neither voice, nor any to answer, nor any that regarded.

30 And Elijah said unto all the people: 'Come near unto me'; and all the people came near unto him. And he repaired the altar of the LORD that was thrown down. **31** And Elijah took twelve stones, according to the number of the tribes of the sons of Jacob, unto whom the word of the LORD came, saying: 'Israel shall be thy name.' **32** And with the stones he built an altar in the name of the LORD; and he made a trench about the altar, as great as would contain two measures of seed. **33** And he put the wood in order, and cut the bullock in pieces, and laid it on the wood.

34 And he said: 'Fill four jars with water, and pour it on the burnt-offering, and on the wood.' And he said: 'Do it the second time'; and they did it the second time. And he said: 'Do it the third time'; and they did it the third time. **35** And the water ran round about the altar; and he filled the trench also with water. **36** And it came to pass at the time of the offering of the evening offering, that Elijah the prophet came near, and said: 'O LORD, the God of Abraham, of Isaac, and of Israel, let it be known this day that Thou art God in Israel, and that I am Thy servant, and that I have done all these things at Thy word. **37** Hear me, O LORD, hear me, that this people may know that Thou, LORD, art God, for Thou didst turn their heart backward.'

38 Then the fire of the LORD fell, and consumed the burnt-offering, and the wood, and the stones, and the dust, and licked up the water that was in the trench. **39** And when all the people saw it, they fell on their faces; and they said: 'The LORD, He is God; the LORD, He is God.' **40** And Elijah said unto them: 'Take the prophets of Baal; let not one of them escape.' And they took them; and Elijah brought them down to the brook Kishon, and slew them there. **41** And Elijah said unto Ahab: 'Get thee up, eat and drink; for there is the sound of abundance of rain.' **42** So Ahab went up to eat and to drink. And Elijah went up to the top of Carmel; and he bowed himself down upon the earth, and put his face between his knees. **43** And he said to his servant: 'Go up now, look toward the sea.' And he went up, and looked, and said: 'There is nothing.' And he said: 'Go again seven times.'

44 And it came to pass at the seventh time, that he said: 'Behold, there ariseth a cloud out of the sea, as small as a man's hand.' And he said: 'Go up, say unto Ahab: Make ready thy chariot, and get thee down, that the rain stop thee not.' **45** And it came to pass in a little while, that the heaven grew black with clouds and wind, and there was a great rain. And Ahab rode, and went to Jezreel. **46** And the hand of the LORD was on Elijah; and he girded up his loins, and ran before Ahab to the entrance of Jezreel.

1 Kings Chapter 19

1 And Ahab told Jezebel all that Elijah had done, and withal how he had slain all the prophets with the sword. **2** Then Jezebel sent a messenger unto Elijah, saying, So let the gods do to me, and more also, if I make not thy life as the life of one of them by to morrow about this time. **3** And when he saw that, he arose, and went for his life, and came to Beersheba, which belongeth to Judah, and left his servant there.

4 But he himself went a day's journey into the wilderness, and came and sat down under a juniper tree: and he requested for himself that he might die; and said, It is enough; now, O LORD, take away my life; for I am not better than my fathers. **5** And as he lay and slept under a juniper tree, behold, then an angel touched him, and said unto him, Arise and eat. **6** And he looked, and, behold, there was a cake baken on the coals, and a cruse of water at his head. And he did eat and drink, and laid him down again. **7** And the angel of the LORD came again the second time, and touched him, and said, Arise and eat; because the journey is too great for thee.

8 And he arose, and did eat and drink, and went in the strength of that meat forty days and forty nights unto Horeb the mount of God.

Bibliography

Bauer, M., & Balius, F. (1995). Storytelling: Integrating therapy and curriculum for students with serious emotional disturbances. *Teaching Exceptional Children 27*(2), 24–28.

Bialik, H. N., & Ravnitzky, Y. H. (Eds.) (1992). *The Book of Legends (Sefer Ha-Aggadah): Legends from the Talmud and the Midrash* (W. J. Braude, Trans.). New York, NY: Schocken Books.

Brown, E. F. (1975). *Bibliotherapy and Its Widening Applications*. Metuchen, NJ: Scarecrow Press.

Coon, C. (2004). *Books to Grow With: A Guide to Using the Best Children's Fiction for Everyday Issues and Tough Challenges*. Portland, OR: Lutra Press.

Coon, C. (2005). *Books to Grow With: A Guide to Using the Best Children's Fiction for Pre-teens — Everyday Issues and Tough Challenges*. Portland, OR: Lutra Press.

Cornett, C. E., & Cornett, C. F. (1980). *Bibliotherapy: The Right Book at the Right Time*. Bloomington, IN: Phi Delta Kappa Educational Foundation.

Darley, J. M. & Latane, B. (1968) Bystander intervention in emergencies: Diffusion of responsibility. *Journal of Personality and Social Psychology 8*(4, Pt.1), 377-383.

Elias, M. J., Tobias, S. E., & Friedlander, B. S. (2000). *Emotionally Intelligent Parenting, How to Raise a Self-Disciplined, Responsible, Socially Skilled Child*. New York, NY: Random House.

Goleman, D. (1995). *Emotional Intelligence*. New York, NY: Bantam Books.

Goleman, D. (2006). *Social Intelligence. The New Science of Human Relationships*. New York, NY: Random House.

Hankin, V., Omer, D., Elias, M., & Raviv, A. (2012). *The Talking Treasure: Stories to Help Build Resilience in Children*. Champaign, IL: Research Press.

The Holy Scriptures According to the Masoretic Text. (1955). Philadelphia, PA: The Jewish Publication Society of America.

Kaplan, K. J. (2012). *Living Biblically: Ten Guides for Fulfillment and Happiness*. Eugene, OR: WIPF and STOCK.

Kaplan, K. J. (1998). *TILT: Teaching Individuals to Live Together*. Philadelphia, PA: Brunner/Mazel.

Kaplan, K. J., & Schwartz. M. B. (2006, 2008). *The Seven Habits of the Good Life: How the Biblical Virtues Free Us from the Seven Deadly Sins*. Lanham, MD: Rowman and Littlefield.

Kaplan, K. J., & Schwartz, M. B. (2008). *A Psychology of Hope: A Biblical Response to Tragedy and Suicide*. Grand Rapids, MI: Wm. B. Eerdmans.

Kaplan, K. J., Schwartz, M. W., & Markus-Kaplan, M. (1984). *The Family: Biblical and Psychological Foundations*. New York, NY: Human Sciences Press.

McCarty, H., & Chalmers, L. (1997). Bibliotherapy: Intervention and prevention. *Teaching Exceptional Children 29*(6), 12–13, 16–17.

Olson, H. D. (1975). Bibliotherapy to help children solve problems. *Elementary School Journal 75*(7), 422–429.

Pardeck, J. (1995). Bibliotherapy: An innovative approach for helping children. *Early Child Development and Care 110*, 83–88.

Schrank, F. A. (1982). Bibliotherapy as an elementary school counseling tool. *Elementary School Guidance and Counseling 16*(3), 218–227.

Schwartz, H. (2004, 2007). *Tree of Souls: The Mythology of Judaism*. New York and Oxford: Oxford University Press.

Schwartz, M. B., & Kaplan, K. J. (2004). *Biblical Stories for Psychotherapy and Counseling: A Sourcebook*. Binghamton, NY: The Haworth Pastoral Press.

Schwartz, M. B., & Kaplan, K. J. (2007). *The Fruit of Her Hands: A Psychology of Biblical Woman*. Grand Rapids, MI: Wm. B. Eerdmans.

Sridhar, D., & Vaughn, S. (2000). Bibliotherapy for all: Enhancing reading comprehension, self-concept, and behavior. *Teaching Exceptional Children 33*(2), 74–82.

Wellisch, E. (1954). *Isaac and Oedipus: A Study in Biblical Psychology of the Sacrifice of Isaac: The Akedah*. London, England: Routledge and Kegan Paul.

About the Authors

Vered Hankin, Ph.D., is Research Assistant Professor at the Department of Medical Social Sciences at Northwestern University's Feinberg School of Medicine. She is also an internationally acclaimed storyteller. As both psychologist and storyteller, Vered lectures and performs nationally and internationally in academic conferences, theaters, charitable organizations, and radio and television. She has been named "the leading storyteller of her generation" (Howard Schwartz, *The Jewish Week*). Her books include *The Talking Treasure: Stories to Help Build Resilience in Children* (with Devorah Omer, Maurice J. Elias, and Amiram Raviv, 2012). Vered's CD recording, *The Day the Rabbi Disappeared: Jewish Holiday Tales of Magic*, based on Howard Schwartz's National Jewish Book Award-winning collection, received the prestigious Award of Excellence from the Film Advisory Board, as well as The Gold Award from NAPPA (National Association of Parenting Publication Awards). Vered joined celebrities Jerry Stiller and others in an internationally aired radio show and audio CD of children's folktales, *One People: Many Stories*. In addition to her storytelling escapades, Vered is also founder and Director of MBSR Chicago, an organization devoted to relaxation interventions for chronic illness. She lives in Chicago with her husband, Jeremy Kaufman, and their three children: Jonah, Coral and Julian. Her work can be followed on www.veredhankin.com and www.mbsrchicago.org

Kalman J. Kaplan, Ph.D., is Professor of Clinical Psychology and Director of the Program in Religion, Spirituality and Mental Health in the Department of Psychiatry and the Department of Medical Education at the University of Illinois at Chicago College of Medicine and an Adjunct Professor at Spertus Institute of Jewish Studies. He has been Editor of the *Journal of Psychology and Judaism* and has published widely in the area of Biblical Psychology. Dr. Kaplan is a Fellow in the American Psychological Association and was a recipient of a 2006–2007 and 2010–2011 Fulbright Fellowship at Tel Aviv University and a 2007–2010 start-up grant from The John Templeton Foundation to develop an online program in Religion, Spirituality, and Mental Health (www.kalmankaplan.com). Dr. Kaplan has recently developed a Hebrew-subtitled version of this program. Among Dr. Kaplan's books are *Living with Schizophrenia* (1997), *TILT: Teaching Individuals to Live Together* (1998), *Right to Die versus Sacredness of Life* (2000), *Biblical Stories for Psychotherapy and Counseling: A Sourcebook* (2004), *The Seven Habits of the Good Life: How the Biblical Virtues Free Us from the Seven Deadly Sins* (2006), *The Fruit of Her Hands: A Psychology of Biblical Woman* (2007), *A Psychology of Hope: A Biblical Response to Tragedy and Suicide* (2008), *Living Biblically: Ten Guides for Fulfillment and Happiness* (2012), and *Politics in the Hebrew Bible: God, Man and Government* (2013, in press). He has also published over 100 articles and chapters in professional journals and books and has lectured widely both nationally and internationally..

Amiram Raviv, Ph.D., is a school and clinical psychologist. He is dean of the School of Psychology at The Center for Academic Studies at Or Yehuda Israel and professor emeritus at the Psychology Department, Tel Aviv University, Israel, where he has served as department chair. Amiram is co-author of the Hebrew books *Crisis and Change in the Life of the Child and His/Her Family, The Israel Parents' Guide,* and *Grandparenting Today,* as well as co-editor of *Peace, Conflict and War: International Perspectives on the Development of Their Understanding by Children and Adolescents,* published in English. He has also published over 100 articles and chapters in professional journals and books. In addition to his academic pursuits, he has been active in various areas of primary prevention, serving as consultant for a number of parenting websites and children's books. He most recently authored *The Talking Treasure: Stories to Help Build Resilience in Children* (with Vered Hankin, Devorah Omer, and Maurice J. Elias, 2012). Amiram has served for more than 15 years as a consultant for the Israeli Educational Television Network on various programs providing counseling to parents. He is married, with two daughters and five grandchildren.

This book is typeset in Adobe Garamond, a digital interpretation of the roman types of Claude Garamond and the italic types of his assistant Robert Granjon designed in the 1540s. Released in 1989, Adobe Garamond type designer Robert Slimbach has captured the beauty and balance of the original Garamond typefaces while creating a typeface family that offers all the advantages of a contemporary digital type family. Garamond is considered to be among the most legible and readable serif typefaces for use in print and has also been noted to be one of the most eco-friendly fonts when it comes to ink usage.